Breakup

the end
of a love story

Doubleday

New York   London   Toronto   Sydney   Auckland

Breakup

the end
of a love story

Catherine Texier

PUBLISHED BY DOUBLEDAY
a division of Bantam Doubleday Dell Publishing Group, Inc.
1540 Broadway, New York, New York 10036

DOUBLEDAY and the portrayal of an anchor with a dolphin are trademarks of
Doubleday, a division of Bantam Doubleday Dell Publishing Group, Inc.

BOOK DESIGN BY TERRY KARYDES

Library of Congress Cataloging-in-Publication Data

Texier, Catherine.
Breakup / Catherine Texier. — 1st ed.   p.   cm.
1. Texier, Catherine—Marriage.   2. Women authors, American—20th century—
Biography.   3. Marriage—United States.   I. Title.
PS3570.E96Z89   1998
818′.5403—dc21
[B]   97-32922   CIP

ISBN: 0-385-49268-5

Printed in the United States of America

August 1998

FIRST EDITION

1   2   3   4   5   6   7   8   9   10

For Céline and Chloé, my daughters

and

For Denise Boucher, who said to me:

"you are a writer, you must write this story"

In the middle of the journey of our life I came to myself in a dark wood where the straight way was lost.

Dante
THE DIVINE COMEDY, *Inferno, Canto I*

1

I will never forgive you. I don't love you anymore. I will never make love to you again.

*S*ometimes it's best to perform the surgery without anesthesia, a clean cut, in and out, not a drop of blood, carve out the cancer.

Sometimes the most cruel words hit home like a bullet.

Sometimes the most cruel words are the most merciful.

*T*his morning, when I empty the dishwasher, the pastel-colored Fiestaware sings in the gray light of a rainy morning. The café au lait in the bowl tastes of France. The yellow of the enamel table, the turquoise of the Naugahyde chairs. The bleached-blond maple of the kitchen cabinets. Colors and textures that I love, that I have picked myself. The solidity of the morning ritual.

And if you died, if this were the ultimate loss, wouldn't the taste and colors of the morning be the same, wouldn't the light still pour in from the window; wouldn't the ivy-covered wall across the yard still be there, freeze-framed?

*W*hen you became a father to Juliet, I found in you the father that I never had and I adored you. I adored you for the tenderness with which you touched her, I adored you when you changed her diapers, cooked dinner for her, took her to the doctor, held her in your arms as the plastic surgeon sewed her severed finger back while I was home giving an interview. Did you ever resent taking care of her so much? Maybe you did. We used to say Juliet had two mothers. Sometimes I thought you were the better mother. When Juliet had a temper tantrum and screamed and rolled over on her back and kicked up her legs, you knew how to soothe her better than I did. In spite of your violent temper, you were the most tender father. When you held Juliet against your chest, it was as if I was curled into a father's arms.

I do not feel much anger at this instant. My overwhelming feeling is sadness and mourning, as if you had suddenly died, or our love had crashed in a freak accident.

Our love, the fuel that kept us going for eighteen years go go go without ever looking back: our bodies irresistible to each other, the move from LA to Montreal, from Montreal to New York, the adventure of renovating the apartment, the birth of the girls, forceps for Juliet, who wouldn't come out fast enough. How does it feel to be a mother, asked the doctor in the Montreal hospital. I didn't know. I cried over Juliet's tiny body when I realized she would die one day. That giving birth is also giving death. Lola: the contractions while we were walking outside NYU Hospital along the FDR Drive, with each set leaning on a different tree, panting against your chest, the smell of your leather jacket in my nose. Our love: the manuscripts piling near our computers, reading each other's pages every day. Editing the magazine: up and down the stairs, night and day, running the printers, eating sandwiches on the fly in the old Chevette in between dropping off bundles at the bookstores. Our love: parties and readings and breastfeedings and books, and never enough money. Your fear, your constant fear about money. Sex and fights and making up and little girls' bodies slipping between us in the middle of the night and smelling sugary and tart and keeping us warm. Tiny bridges connecting our flesh.

The density of that life, the particular color and taste of it, its thickness, its furious liveliness, I wouldn't know how to find words to describe it. Only that it has filled me, that I've been overflowing with it. That it is messy and crude and raw and that it reaches deep where souls lurk, deep where old pains lie dormant.

Tomorrow I know the light will shift and we might be filled with tenderness or fatigue. Yes, we'll have battle-fatigue, palming our bowls of café au lait after too little sleep. And at noon, maybe, it'll be peace, light and awkward, fragile, a tiny little bud of new peace with nowhere to go.

If it wasn't for the kids, I wouldn't have been here when you came back from France. I wouldn't be here now.

*A*nother night. Twisting the stiletto sideways for maximum damage.

But why? What happened?

I am so passive-aggressive, you say, I don't understand how you can take it. If I were you I would have booted me out already. I admire what you're doing. Don't think that I am oblivious to that. You're very brave.

I know, I say. It's because I love you.

I am like the welterweight in the ring taking the punishment, taking it and taking it, but standing on her feet. They say about those kinds of boxers that they have heart. I have a lot of heart.

*I*t's 4 or 5 A.M., both of us lying naked on the bed, holding each other. The easy companionship of bodies that know how to make one another come and come and come. I believe in our relationship. I believe that we still have this thing. That, deep down, you still have it for me.

Maybe, you say, brutally honest, or maybe provocative, but I don't feel it.

You're still angry at me, right?

Maybe.

Don't you love this apartment, don't you love coming down for coffee in the morning with me, don't you love what we have?

Yes, you whisper.

But you want to give up the great sex, the great apartment, living with the kids, you want to give up all that?

In answer you get up sullenly and go downstairs to make coffee, and we drink it in silence at the yellow table.

I know you're trying to provoke me to kick you out, but I

won't. If you want to leave, you're going to have to make the decision by yourself. The truth is that I can't bear the idea of you leaving.

But you're not leaving. Not yet anyway. You mutter something about settling the kids in school, waiting for more money.

I don't say anything.

I've heard all that before. In a teleplay, or a bad movie. In real life our dialogues are not as witty and sarcastic as those you write. We're uttering tired lines. Midlife crisis: Act I.

In the dark we hold each other tight.

I can't believe you can take it, you say. In a way it's disgusting.

What's disgusting? I don't understand what you're saying. Maybe you mean *you're* disgusting.

When I put Lola to bed, I hold her tight in the dark and feel as if we are drowning. I want to hold Juliet in my arms too when she goes to sleep, but she declines, too mushy maybe for a fifteen-year-old. Then relents: okay, but you've got to scratch my back. I'm not in the mood for scratching anybody's back. I want arms around me, a cock inside me, fingers playing with me, drawing my juice, your warm mouth on mine, your tongue circling deep around mine, our tongues together, dancing, deep, deep, our bodies falling into the well, losing breath.

You're taking your revenge. Your revenge cannot be satiated. Revenge for what? What did I do?

I will never forgive you. I will never make love with you again. I do not love you anymore.

What did I do to be punished so? What nerve did I touch? How did I do you wrong?

Up and down the stairs, the apartment pitches forward and aft. Shoes on the steps, a pair of pink panties thrown across the hallway, a brown bath towel hanging all twisted on the banister, flyers and manuscripts and newspapers and books, the home of two writers, leaving a continuous trail of paper behind them like two snails. Our life spinning and coming apart in toys and un-identified little objects and detritus blowing past.

I will never forgive you. I will never make love with you again. I do not love you anymore.

*D*id you ever say to me: I will always love you? I can't remem-ber. A little over a year ago, in the summer of 1995, you took me to a little bar on East Ninth Street and told me: you are the woman of my life. And I said: you are the man of my life. We kissed passionately, our knees entwined. And I still feel the same today, even if your love has suddenly dissolved.

*L*ook at his picture of me, you say, showing me one of your new publicity shots, a close-up of your wild head of curls and a wicked smile. Look at this: I look like I'm sixteen in it.

I cringe a little, not wanting to allow you the pleasure of your vanity. And you look like a kid, yes, it's true, like that teenager you've almost always looked like, gangly and graceful and hard and tender—not entirely grown man.

*Y*ou've just come back from biking to the Jersey shore, on your brand-new, cherry-red BMW 750, and it looks as if your determi-nation to break up is back stronger. You have withdrawn again. The wall is up. Here you come, in the front door, closed face, rigid chest, tight shoulders, your mood engulfing me, drawing me into your script of doom.

And yet there's comfort, also, in the familiarity of your body swaying down the hallway, the gesture of hanging your hat on a peg.

I panic. Don't shut me out! Don't shut me out! As if the oxygen has been abruptly cut off. Thrown off center again, struggling to find my footing in the middle of the battle: your anger like black clouds under your forehead, dark dark, and you standing up rigidly, defying me.

I am supposed to crumble, but I don't.

This is your way: withdrawing into rigid anger, cutting off all communication, but instead of coming out of it after a couple of days or a week or two, like you used to, you're stuck there. Like a giant acting up, a temper tantrum of mega proportions.

Am I to be the sacrificial lamb, the victim of a ritual, psychic killing, slaughtered on the altar of your ego?

The object of your rage and your blame?

I feel trapped in a hallucinatory scenario, your anger fixated on me, the words *I do not love you anymore; I do not feel anything for you anymore* repeated without variation, obsessively, ruthless honesty bordering on sadism, as if we were now caught into a new game, torturer and victim, under the utterance of a simple, unemotional, declaration of fact.

*Y*esterday I held you in my arms and I said: I love you, I know you're going through a major crisis, and I accept it.

Yeah, you said, I'm going through a crisis. And you repeated, again, lest I might have forgotten: I'm only here because of the children. I am still leaning toward leaving rather than not.

Are you open to the possibility that you might change your mind? I asked you. And you said yes.

I went to pick up Lola and when I came back we talked some

more. You said: I don't want to go back to that shit we were in before I took the job, we were both depressed, then when I started working, I finally got out of it and I felt like you wanted to pull me back with you in the house, you didn't want to let me go.

Why didn't you tell me? I said.

You got defensive.

But I did.

Not like that.

You looked away.

I was afraid you would crumble, fall apart, you said. I didn't think I could talk to you, I saw you as this pale, fragile creature who couldn't take anything.

There are a lot of things I didn't say to you either, I said. I was afraid you'd fly into a rage.

After that we were silent for a while.

At night, in a half sleep, you took me in your arms, and when you fully woke up, turned your back to me.

Sometimes I feel so rejected, like when you fell asleep on Juliet's bed because you so obviously didn't want to lie down and read next to me on our bed, that my stomach churns and I want to throw up. Throw up the pain.

Sometimes I think I should be the one who leaves. I am the one who doesn't belong, the wanderer, the foreigner. Go back to France, travel. Live in Paris again, or in Latin America. Roam the jungles of Vietnam or the Ivory Coast. There's something wrong in this picture, you leaving. I am the restless one, the one who can't stay still. I've been stable all these years because of you. Or was it the opposite: you were stable because of me. All I know is that we've been each other's anchor.

Your unhappiness: a cloak of lead on the house. But at times, too, there's a lightness, a surprising warmth resurfacing from an earlier time, as if what was between us refuses to die.

We maintain the discipline of a family ruled by the kids' schedule and the meals. Up at 7 A.M., girls driven to school, coming back in the afternoon, homework, dinner, food shopping on weekends.

There's hardly any flesh left on our life, the bare bones are already sticking through the skin.

——

*S*omething has changed between us. You've pulled the plug. Hold it, you said. I've had it. We were caught in some shit, some vicious taunting, cat and mouse game, and now the jig is up.

The hero moves on to another adventure, freed of his chains, leaving the heroine behind to crawl into a corner and die. Or to stand up as a martyr, cloaked in her haunting weakness. Maybe she has a nervous breakdown. Is committed to an insane asylum, nineteenth-century style, like Camille Claudel after her breakup with Rodin. He went on creating powerful sculptures and she never set foot again in her studio.

I wouldn't write a story like that, I would find it laughable, full of exhausted clichés. Passé. I wouldn't read it either. I refuse to live it.

This is the story I would tell: the hero needs to spread his wings, free himself, test himself, renew himself. The heroine freaks and puts the screws on him. The hero flees. End of first act. The heroine comes back on stage: okay, I hear you. You've been wounded, you need space, so do I. The story goes on. But it's now about something else. There's death and resurrection. The second act is only starting.

Your story leaves me no room at all, no other option than to accept the ritual killing of me—the wife—so that the liberated hero can fly off on his own.

Is my story better than yours? I don't know. All I know is that I am not going to play the part you've assigned me.

———

*W*ent to Spy tonight with an Australian friend. Got drunk on whiskey sours. Talked about women's sexuality and obsessions. Came back raging at you and wanting to fuck so badly, how can you not want to fuck, how can you take it? Forget about that *I don't love you anymore* bullshit. So what? Let's make love anyway. What's the difference? Haven't you ever fucked women you didn't love? I would understand it if you had a girlfriend, that would make sense. If you had another woman under the skin.

And maybe you do.

Maybe you do.

The day you told me you didn't love me anymore I asked you if there was something else going on in your life.

It was an oblique question. I didn't have the nerve to ask you point-blank: are you having an affair? Because that word, affair, was unmentionable. Because to imagine you involved with someone else was unthinkable. Because you and me . . . You and me . . . We've been everything together. We've had the relationship that everyone dreams of.

So I gave you an out, and you took it. You got testy, you said: *that's* what's going on in my life, meaning: your anger at me, meaning: your desire to leave me. And I didn't push it.

You're humiliating me, you know that? Staying for the kids. What bullshit is that? You're supposed to be a bad guy, a tough guy. Why don't you pack up your bags and leave? What a wuss! So you don't fuck me, that's my punishment, isn't it? Let's see how long that's going to last. Meanwhile, you come back for dinner, stay with the girls. You make Lola's lunch box, you take her to school on your bicycle, you spend more time with them than you have in a long time. You hang out at home. So virtuous, such a good, responsible guy.

You know I love you, don't you? Compassion is what you said you felt for me. *Compassion!* Fuck your compassion. I don't want your pity. If it wasn't for the kids, I would leave too, spit in your face, how dare you, how dare you reject me. You're killing me, you're killing our love, our passion. And for what? You think I fucked you over, but don't you see you're destroying a part of yourself too?

> *Parfois la paix descend*
> *et la tendresse de te voir si ouvert,*
> *tes yeux où tremble une âme trouble,*
> *un petit creux une flamme qui passe*
> *qui ne m'est pas destinée*
> *mais que je prends au passage*
> *parce qu'elle me réchauffe*
> *le coeur*
> *et je la prends à la dérobée*
> *et je la savoure,*
> *la tiens*
> *au creux de mes mains*
> *aussi longtemps*
> *qu'elle brûle*
> *nous nous la repassons*
> *comme une balle*

tu es mon complice
à ton corps défendant.

I wrote this poem for you after a talk we had about Abbie Hoffman. You were saying Abbie Hoffman was a good Jewish boy who wanted to be bad. And I said: just like you, right? And you made that smirk you make: wry, self-deprecating, half-conceding, half-revealing, half-concealing. Like you.

I wrote the poem in French. I haven't written in French in a long time. I also don't usually write poetry. Maybe the occasion called for French poetry. I don't know. The poem is about tenderness and complicity. The poem is about you. But you won't understand it. A little maybe. All these classes at the Alliance Française haven't really paid off.

Do you remember? I started to write in English so that you could read me.

I feel your moods like changing weather on a boat. I can read them on your face. Tough/vulnerable/open/close. Sometimes going back and forth in a split second. You're always tightly coiled, ready to take off like a rocket. And I pull on the sails to adjust. But you adjust to me too. It's a kind of dance we perform, aware of each other.

Your dark, fuck-you mood, when you were getting ready to go out for dinner and you noticed I was watching you.

You going out?

I *told* you I was going out.

A little testy. Accent on the told.

Yes, I said, you did.

Stirring the shrimp and pea risotto I was making, on the off chance you might stay, although you had mentioned earlier you might go out to dinner, but I had decided to make it anyway because I felt like cooking. Did I possibly hope to hold you back with my cooking? How low can I get? Which is lower: to try to keep you with my cooking or with sex?

They say you should stand in the eye of the storm, and let it rage around you. Is that what we are doing? Waiting out the storm?

Except the storm is raging inside. We do not fight. (I am afraid of your rage.) We talk, a little. We tiptoe around our feelings.

We make love.

So much for *I will never make love to you anymore.*

I am calm (I hide the panic).

You are the one in crisis. Torn, you said. Poised to destroy everything.

———

I want to measure myself, you say, see what I am worth on my own. You also say: the last few years, you made me think of my mother, pulling on me emotionally, dragging me down.

Your mother! Me!

Last year, when you were going out all the time, you made me think of my own mother. Running out at night to meet her lovers, her friends, running off because she was suffocating at home, the home of my grandparents. Always running out the door. And the door slamming behind her. Leaving me behind.

So you've turned me into your mother. And I've turned you into mine.

If only we could have a good laugh about that. But nobody's laughing.

Your body, flung at the extreme edge of the bed to avoid me, but sometimes coming into my arms with a sigh. Your freckled back lit up in the dim light of your lamp when you can't sleep, your shoulders tight, hunched over, your back a carapace, a porcupine with its sharp needles sticking outward, spitting poison in my direction.

And me, finally falling asleep. Letting myself go through the mattress, grateful for the softness of the bed, the warmth of the comforter.

I don't want to romanticize it, you say.

Romanticize what? What are you talking about? Romanticize your desire to leave? I thought *we* were romantic.

You say: I want you to be fully yourself.

You say: I have very deep feelings toward you.

You say: we have this sexual chemistry between us that will always be there. But emotionally and intellectually I am shut down.

You also say: if you had pulled yourself together a year ago . . .

Why: "a year ago"? What happened a year ago?

Your words are sibylline.

A year ago I spent the month of August in France at my mother's house with Juliet and Lola. A year ago I met my father for the first time in my life in a little restaurant in Provence. A year ago you got laid off from your job. A year ago your behavior began to change: you took the habit of returning videotapes after dinner while I was putting Lola to bed and not coming home until 2 A.M.; you left for the supermarket on Sunday mornings and didn't come back until 4 or 5 P.M. When I asked you where you had been, you said: I went out for a drink, or I had to do some errands, or I went out to watch the ballgame. If I insisted, you said: don't cling to me. I don't have to answer to you.

A year ago, I began to lose you.

But when you say: "if you had pulled yourself together," I know you refer to my emotional troubles, the anxieties and panic attacks that plagued me when Juliet fell ill with a blood disorder called ITP, eight years ago. For three hellish months we were in the hospital with her three times a week to monitor her platelet count while she was on prednisone. She eventually recovered, but those three months were the scariest time of my life. Soon after that my mother had a heart attack and I started a psychotherapy. It was supposed to last only a few months, but it's still going on. I know you think that I am still not "myself," or "the way I used to be".

But I can't look back now and regret the years of depression and confusion and no money. What happened, happened. Cannot be relived, cannot be redone differently. And there are wounds that can't be healed and wounds that can be. And who's to know beforehand which are which.

Maybe there's been a breakdown of trust, you say. And I don't really know what you mean, but I believe that maybe trust can be rebuilt.

I am accumulating parking tickets at an alarming rate. Five since I came back, including one in Hempstead, where I teach creative writing at Hofstra University, due to having parked off campus one day when I arrived an hour late on a rainy morning. Otherwise, things are functioning fairly smoothly, during the week at least, when I am busy with the writing and the teaching.

But the weekends turn into blurs of pain, maybe because they are symbolic of family life. I float on your moods, going up and down, afraid to drown, to be sucked into the black hole. You disappear the whole afternoon on Saturdays, sometimes the whole day on Sundays. You're never here on Saturday nights. I don't ask any questions anymore. I don't have to answer to you, you tell me. But I think I don't want to hear the answers. I stay alone with the girls. Lola screams for food, for a cassette to be popped into the VCR. Juliet opens my door and bangs it in fury because I'm staying on the phone too long.

The three of us are trapped in this house and we take out our rage on each other. The family dynamics are turning into the law of the jungle. And I am caught, paralyzed in the chain of fear.

I know my rage should be directed at you, but I am terrified to confront you head-on. I am still clinging to those little shreds of love you toss me.

The rage of being rejected. It's one thing to be with a guy and see that he's losing interest and maybe you are too, and quite another to have built a family and two literary careers and a house and eighteen years of shared companionship, the passion still going full swing in spite of the mounting tensions, and to feel the plug being pulled out overnight without warning.

Like being shot in the back by a cop.

I didn't know, you said, I didn't know I would find myself on the edge so fast. For a long time the edge seemed far away, then all of a sudden the edge was right here.

─────

$\mathcal{T}$he afternoon sun pours into my office windows and the rows of books on the bookcases are calm and steady, the framed photographs quiet, the bowl of tea reassuring, my desk cleaned up. Life suspended for a brief moment.

I thought I had the space, the time to reconstruct myself. A psychotherapy is a long journey. It makes you regress, it inhibits you. It makes you pull inward. Maybe, as you say, I became too self-involved. Maybe I did lose myself. But I thought you would wait for me. I thought we had that kind of love. Unconditional love, like mother love. You can fuck up and be forgiven. I didn't think I had done you wrong. In eighteen years I hadn't been with another man, I hadn't run away from home, I hadn't drunk myself blind, I hadn't taken drugs, street or prescription. Okay, yeah, I am neurotic. I admit it. You got sick of my hypochondria and panic attacks and inarticulate fears and various compulsions and obsessions, but hey, I thought we had a deal: you put up with my anxieties, I put up with your depressions.

You are codependent, you told me.

Brain-dead.

Do you realize the last few years you were brain-dead?

This house is hysterical, you said.

I thought it was lively.

Chaotic, but never boring.

You got tired of being two writers in the same house, cut off from the outside world. You felt we were drowning. When you finally took a job, your mood lifted. Within six months you were going out almost every night, or if you were showing up it was to put your feet under the table and complain about the food or about the kids fighting.

Overnight we had turned into a parody of a bad marriage.

But I wanted to believe everything was alright. You kept telling me you were happy to live with me, that you had never been bored with me a second, that you loved everything about our life.

And I believed you. I so wanted to believe you.

—————

I dreamed last night that you were leaving, but you were not leaving our apartment. We were staying in a suburban house that looked like the one you grew up in on Long Island, and our bed had this flowered yellow bedspread matching the curtains and the wallpaper. I was lying in bed with Juliet, who was about ten in the dream, and all your luggage was spread out in the bedroom and around the house. All over the place, there were these huge clothes bags and duffel bags already packed and stuffed, old baggage from your college days, baggage that I didn't even know you had, that I had never seen. You didn't leave in my dream. You were still home in the morning, and I was still lying in this flowered bed, surrounded by all your stuff.

Before the dream, during the evening, you were raging at me: you said that our relationship had turned claustrophobic and that you had wanted to have a separate social life from me, but it didn't mean, then, that you had wanted to leave, you never thought it would be a problem. You said I couldn't handle anything and that I was falling apart all the time.

I listened to you, lying on my back. You were not looking at me. You were sitting on the side of the bed, your back to me and

I could see your muscles tensing, your shoulders hunched, and one time you got up to go to the bathroom. Our relationship has become sick, you said on your way back, and I kept staring at your naked hip and thigh, I didn't want to see your face.

You got back into bed, still not looking at me, still shaking with rage.

I had no idea you had such resentment against me, I said. You kept saying you loved me.

I don't have any patience with this anymore.

Do you think I am falling apart now? I asked you.

You got angry again.

How would *I* know?

Am I falling apart now?

I don't know, you said. I think you're just disguising it.

———

Yesterday you told Juliet you were only staying because of her and Lola. Juliet asked you: do you still love Mom? And you said: I don't know.

This morning you apologized to her and said you didn't mean to scare her.

———

We went to a screenplay reading yesterday. Our first public outing since I came back from France. I didn't know if we were going as a couple or as . . . as what? Is there a word for what we are? I was sitting on a chair waiting for you to get me a drink.

After a while I got up to look for you. You were at the bar, talking to two women, one the producer who had inadvertently caused the beginning of our fatal last fight in July.

We met at the Bowery Bar, the producer said to me.

Oh, I said, looking into her eyes, yes, and I smiled. I thought life was ironical. What about my beer, I asked you.

Here, you said, and you handed it to me, smiling.

You and me smiling those fake social smiles to cover up the abyss between us. I hung out with you for a while. Then I moved away from the bar, not wanting to intrude, and I saw you lean to kiss the producer on the cheek. Bye, girl, you said. Confident, flirtatious, a player.

And I knew what had terrified me then, why I had clung to you so ferociously, trying to pull you back to me. The fear of losing you to the world. And I understood your rage at me for trying to hold you back to our little world of the two of us, that world you said had become suffocating. I watched you play the room, nod and kiss and talk about your next projects, wearing your new soft black hat, your hip-hop/biker cool look. I remembered how shy you had been years ago, hanging back with me. How shy the both of us had been. And I realized at that instant how scared and insecure I still was, still hanging back. And I saw that you needed to take your distance, that you were like a butterfly coming out of your cocoon and trying out your wings, and that I represented the cocoon that you'd come out of. I felt cold and exposed, utterly naked, taking shaky steps into a world where you had already grown confident. And I knew that I had to dive in, that I couldn't cling to you anymore, that I didn't have the choice, that there was no turning back.

Later on, in the middle of the night, I felt your hard cock brush against my hand like it does, when you're in a half sleep—your body wanting me while your mind resists—and you turned your back to me, but I could feel you still wanted me. I wasn't sure if I wanted you because I've had to shut down my feelings, too, to protect myself, but you pulled me to you and sat me on your face and I felt your mouth open my cunt lips like you love to do and I placed your hands on my tits and you started to play with my nipples while you were eating me, sucking me off till I came into your mouth with deep grunts and I slid down your chest and you were soft and I played with you with my mouth and my fingers till you got hard again. But when I tried to kiss you, you pulled your face to the side, not wanting to give me your lips, not wanting to give me your love, and I said: it's okay, baby, it's okay. And you let go inside of me right away. I dismounted you and went to pee, but when I came back you'd turned your back to me again. So I cradled you in my arms and you curled your body inside of mine. And we fell asleep together.

The air is cool now, late September early morning air, pure and light, the summer softening, folding into the ripening of fall, a gentleness to soothe my open wounds, our ailing relationship now wide open, oozing pus and blood on the operating table.

I've been back for a whole month.

Your arms around me, your cock stirring against my thighs. Not only because you are horny, I think, but because you're letting go of something. Your body tucked against mine. Searching mine. My arms encircling you. It isn't just about sex this time, no overt eroticism. But a deeper need, reaching out through the layers of anger and frustration, our bodies looking for closeness, for each other, like they always have, like fishes underwater in the dark.

———

*I*t's not about fucking other women, you said. Our sexual chemistry will never go away.

————

I pulled four hamburgers out of the freezer and laid them on the counter next to three ears of corn we'd just gotten with the box of organic vegetables that gets delivered every Wednesday, and when you came down from your office upstairs—it was around 6:30 P.M.—and saw the four hamburgers, you said, coldly: I'm not having dinner here tonight.

I feel a little twinge but not more than that because that's our new, unspoken deal: total freedom and no questions asked. So I say, okay, and put one hamburger back into the freezer. And right after that I feel fine: this is the deal, my deal with you anyway, because I don't think you've got a deal with me. What you have is an attitude, I-bet-you-can't-pull-it-off attitude, I'm-waiting-for-my-next-paycheck-and-I'm-outta-here attitude. I lay down on the couch next to the girls, who are watching an old rerun of "Blossom" on TV, and tell them: it's just the three of us having dinner tonight, your dad is going out, how soon do you want to eat? And Juliet says she's hungry and asks for sautéed potatoes, and I get up to start them.

Around sevenish, I see you getting ready, putting your shoes on, a shirt over your T-shirt, preparing your briefcase—so this is going to be a work dinner—and all of a sudden you tell me about several film deals that are about to go down. All the details spill out, and I want to hold you in my arms and kiss you. I am stupidly happy, not so much happy about the film deals, but happy about your opening up to me, that we still have that little thread of a connection. Does that mean we'll be swimming in money? I ask, as if we are still going to be together, you and I, when these deals come through, climbing the social ladder side by side. You say, I don't know about that.

I know you must think I am in total denial. And I am, in a way—not just denying—but asserting what I believe, which is that, deep down, we are still together, and acting accordingly.

You let me hold you but didn't hold me back.

So I stepped away, and went back to preparing dinner. When you were ready to go out you went to the couch to kiss the girls good night, and on the way out you brushed my waist with your hand.

Maybe you were grateful, amazed, even, that I was letting you go, no strings attached. It wasn't entirely self-sacrificing, masochistic, on my part. When the door closed behind you, a warmth spread inside of me. I felt whole, released. I was glad that you were gone. You were taking the tensions with you. I was glad to be eating dinner alone with Juliet and Lola, just the three of us girls in front of some stupid TV sitcom. I gave a bath to Lola afterward and took her to bed and went to bed myself.

When I woke up it was 1:30 A.M. and I heard the TV downstairs, which you turn on when you come back late at night. A little while later you lay down next to me. I said hey to you and you said hey, but I could feel you had closed up again.

It's as if you had two lives: one outside, and one inside the house, where we are all together, and sometimes the two intersect when we're both invited somewhere. Inside the house our relationship goes on: our daily talks about writing, about the kids, about our work, and sometimes about your overwhelming anger, about your feelings toward me (what's left of them), and about my feelings toward you (I cling to my undying love for you); and we cook and eat dinner together (tonight you made a big pot of tomato sauce) and we sleep together naked in the same bed every night and sometimes we make love, tentatively, protectively, and sometimes I hold you in my arms and sometimes you hold me in your arms, and I can tell that you're not quite there at times, and at other times you let go of your anger or whatever is eating you and your warmth gushes out.

If I asked you again, if I tried to take your emotional temperature, you might—probably would—say that your feelings haven't changed. Which is the reason why I will not ask you. And yet life moves imperceptibly, like waves lapping at a cliff, every minute of peace making its little dent, leaving its print, every minute of peace soothing the wound.

You don't seem scared, my shrink says to me.

But I am terrified, I feel like I'm standing at the edge of a cliff staring into the void. Because I've uprooted myself from my country, you are my home, my heart.

When I flew to New York from Montreal a month after giving birth to Juliet, you had prepared the apartment for us. Among the ladders and the two-by-fours and the bare brick walls in our future bedroom, you had laid out an Oriental rug and a mattress covered with an Indian bedspread and pillows, and you had lit up a candle and set a bottle of chilled white wine and two glasses on the floor. I lay Juliet in her basket outside the room on a steamer trunk, and you took me into your arms.

To me you were the home I never had, your arms and your chest and the perimeter of the kitchen table with your mug of steaming coffee in front of you.

That night, in March 1981, Juliet was one month old. She had fallen asleep in her little basket. You sat down on the bed next to me and handed me a glass of white wine.

Welcome home, baby, you said.

I knew I would always be safe with you. I knew you would never wish me any harm.

This morning at the Union Square greenmarket I had the blues while I was buying eggs and chicken and filling my straw basket with Winesap apples fresh-picked upstate. I had stale memories of the Saturday-morning market, boring, boring, boring, and yet reassuring, in hindsight, as if shopping together had been a ritual asserting the reality of this constantly moving and elusive entity: a family.

It's cool and sunny today. You went biking upstate.

A peace seems to have descended on the house. Maybe the peace is in me. Lying down on the big white couch with a newspaper or a magazine, sitting at my desk and writing, filling out the space, feeling at home when you're not here, not having a clue who I am at this point in my life, and yet feeling that weird sense of peace, after you called me from Saugerties this afternoon, to tell me that you were going to stop somewhere to warm up and would come back later in the night.

The fever has broken and now I can relax, I don't have to prove anything to anyone anymore. I don't have to *do* anything, except what I want. Excited at the coolness of fall, the prospect of wearing heavy sweaters, winter boots, hats, a new year opening up. Feeling free: free to travel, free to think, free to start a new project, free to imagine, free to take chances. Free and scared.

Without you, I am left with myself. Myself, not-the-mother, not-the-lover, not-the-wife, and I am faced with an anonymous, countryless identity.

One of the first things I did, after you told me you wanted to leave, was to buy the biggest French-English dictionary I could find at Barnes & Noble, a Larousse, and to stand it on the shelf near my old, college-days Harrap's. Maybe I had an idea that the key to my identity was my ability to translate the two languages into each other. I had been wanting to buy a new dictionary for years. There had never been a sense of urgency. And now there was.

I can't take care of you anymore, you said, I can't be your mirror anymore, I have no patience for your tears, for your anxieties, for your neediness anymore.

No more? No more leaning on your shoulder, no more hearing your voice, so soft, so tender, telling me, as you did so many times: everything's going to be okay, baby, don't worry?

Thanks, baby, for the bitter pill, thanks for the wake-up call.

And I thought I was the most lovable, vulnerable woman.

Yeah right.

New York, tough city.

Juliet is sleeping over at a friend's in North Salem. I dropped her off at another friend's house on Broadway in the afternoon, they were all going to take the train together at Penn Station. Lola is playing Barbies with her friend Camelia upstairs in the guest room, I can hear them laugh at intervals, high-pitched voices rising above the buzz of the steam heat coming up in the radiator. Reassuring sounds that make me feel safe, connected.

The house doesn't feel like a trap anymore, the space opens up, it becomes fluid, alive.

With Juliet today we wondered if you feel left out when the three of us hang out together. Three French women talking clothes and makeup and tampons and yelling up and down the stairs when you're trying to write or watch the baseball game. In your own family the women knit or cook and chat away while the men sit sullenly in front of the TV or read the newspaper. Maybe you feel this house has become a replica of your original family. I don't know. But I do know that you feel trapped, that your office is going to hell, that you talk for hours on the phone in a barely audible voice. The phone, your lifeline to the outside world.

You want to run. To escape.

I am so troubled right now, you told me, the only time when I feel okay is when I go on the bike, because of the attention it de-

mands. On the motorcycle, your concentration has to be 100 percent, always your eyes on the road, anticipating what's going to happen, your attention can never waver, it would be too dangerous.

When you said, I am so troubled right now, it was like a gift to
me, a confidence. A tiny moment of openness. A tiny moment of
trust. I am living for these little crumbs. And when you came back
for dinner later, we all sat around the coffee table to eat and watch
Diabolique on TV, this atrocious remake of Clouzot's *Les Diaboliques*.
It was the four of us together again, this fragile balance, a music
that we played. And you were here, not elsewhere. And then in
bed, no. You kept to yourself, quiet, reading. You let me hold you
until we fell asleep. That's all.

And yet, a couple of nights ago, the sex was so hot. I barely
touched your thigh and zap, we were in each other's arms. Later,
curled inside your arms I whispered: don't take this away from us.
Sex is a lot more than sex. You are free, I don't want to hold you back.

You didn't say anything. We hugged each other for a while,
and then you turned away.

Tonight you had a business dinner for a film project. You called
me from the restaurant to ask me to drop off your house keys.
You're misplacing your keys all the time. Once you left them on
the motorcycle, in the street. A neighbor brought them back to
me. Another time you dropped your bicycle key on the basement
floor. You lose your keys at about the same rate I get parking
tickets. At the restaurant we chatted for a while about a screening we had all been to earlier. Again, I didn't know if we were
together or not. Subtle back and forth between us, you looking
at me, responding to me, and yet not *with* me.

I was on my way to a reading at a friend's house in Brooklyn. The painful relearning of being alone. Painful, I am beginning to realize, not because I do not enjoy going out on my own, but because it makes me aware of not wearing any mask, of being just me. Surprised, too, to see that I can be myself without effort.

Fiasco last night, going out for drinks with a group of writers, everybody in their late twenties and early thirties. We were supposed to go to a rave, or a jungle party, but we never made it. We ended up drinking in a bar in Tribeca for hours. Then on to another bar on East Fifth Street where some people hit the bathroom for coke. I was bored and had an acute feeling of emptiness. Nobody was going dancing anymore. I came back at 3:30 A.M., slept badly for three or four hours and woke up feeling down. You were cold and hostile in the morning, and I tried to draw you out, but your anger was palpable, snapping between us. In the afternoon you went out to watch the baseball game and came back for dinner. I try to imagine where you go on weekend afternoons to watch the ballgames. I don't think you go to a bar, or to a friend's. What friend? I know of other guys who spend their time in bars. But you never did that.

Where do you go? My mind hits a blank.

At this moment, my place is here, holding the home together, keeping the hearth going, so to speak. It's a traditionally feminine task that I never thought I would take to. Me holding the family together because I still love you, because you're the man of my life, even if you're tortured and unloving right now. Or is it because I am scared? A last-ditched attempt to keep you at any cost? You used to be the one holding the family together. It was your warmth, your passion that made me want to stay in the fold. Still, the homemaker role feels alien to me, forced.

The more I think about it, the more I see that this situation requires a Zen approach: not looking at a goal, but concentrating on the right attitude, day after day, minute after minute, and seizing the moment, knowing intuitively when to move forward, and when not to do anything and let things ride. Keeping my balance no matter what happens.

And finally, a scene from this weekend that I want to report before checking out: I had a flat tire on Saturday morning on my way to picking up Lola at dance class. I pulled the car into a gas station and called you to come and help me. Then when I went back to the car I decided I would give it a shot. I hadn't changed a tire in more than twenty years. But I started working the jack, and this guy who was getting gas jumped out of his van and gave me a hand. By the time you showed up on your bike, it was all done. You seemed relieved that I had taken care of it myself. You just checked to make sure the bolts were tight enough.

Before you left I opened my arms to you and kissed you. You moved your face sideways but I said, come on, and you said, what, and I said, you know I love you. You let me kiss you and then pulled away and muttered something which sounded almost like: me too, but it was so low, so mumbled, so unsaid that I couldn't be sure, but there was a flash of warmth between us and I held on to it all day.

The leaves are changing in the trees in Tompkins Square Park, and on the ivy crawling on the building across my window, green morphing to intense yellow and deep red, a signal that time has passed since I've come back from France, inching toward hard fall and winter. Toward the unknown. A signal that things change and shift all the time. That time does its work.

Your anger: a given, since the morning we woke up together after making love for the first time in Dave's apartment on West Sixty-ninth Street. We were making the bed and you pulled on the comforter a little too hard, testily, for no reason that I could figure out, anger flaring up in your face for a split second out of the blue, unconnected with what we were doing, which was smoothing the comforter on the bed, but I felt it rippling through me, superimposed on your smile and the touch of your lips on mine, like a shot of vodka in cream sauce. It surprised me. But I didn't mind. It added an ingredient of danger, unpredictability.

And now here is your anger again, blown out of proportion, teetering, vindictive, unleashed. Killing rage. Not only directed at me, but at your film agent who hasn't gotten you the screenplays you were up for—not yet anyway, and maybe never. Toward your parents for being old and sick and goddamned needy. Especially toward your mother for crying all the time. Toward yourself maybe? The anger fading sometimes to a dull ache, to a garden-variety anger. As if some days you were just getting tired, your energy flagging. How long can anger last if it isn't fanned, fed? Doesn't a fire burn itself out, eventually, running out of wood? Or can simmering, buried rage be forever rekindled?

One night you said to me: by falling apart and crying you are trying to get something.

By "falling apart and crying" I think you specifically refer to that time last spring when my last novel was turned down the same week you sold your own novel and you found me sobbing at my desk. Or all the other times when I burst into tears at the sight of a rejection letter. Or my obsessions about everybody's health. Even after Juliet completely recovered from her blood disorder, I was so shook-up that for years after that, whenever one of us was sick, I worried that it might be a fatal illness. The spectacle of my vulnerability is odious to you.

You mean, I am being manipulative?

Yes, you said. Manipulative.

It was one of our night talks, 4 A.M., lying down in the dark, side by side.

What was I trying to get from you by playing up my weaknesses, my neediness? Maybe I wanted you to tell me you loved me no matter what, you would forgive me, you would not hurt me, you would always be there for me. Maybe I was afraid to threaten you if I showed you how strong I could be. Maybe I was trying to disarm you.

And you, what are you trying to get with your rage? Is it the rage of the warrior, burning everything in his path, like Attila the Hun? Is it righteous rage, like that of Saint-Just, who, when he finally took power during the French Terror, sent all the former friends that had crossed him to the guillotine? Is it the helpless rage of the child who has developed that foolproof weapon to keep the world at bay? The rage of the rattlesnake firing off its poison when threatened?

They say Pisces take on the problems of the world, they absorb the energy around them, good or bad, they have trouble with boundaries, they need to protect themselves from other people's unbearable intrusion. Is anger your armor, your hard shell, protecting your vulnerable soul?

How the pain comes back, so fast. How your angry silence unsettles me. How helpless I feel, how lonely. How I thought your love was forever, even if we didn't talk that way. How secure I felt in that love until about a year or two ago, when you started acting as if you wanted to fuck every woman you saw.

You did love me. You did shower me with love. You adored me. You told me I was the woman of your life.

Didn't you?

The house, when your mood pitches black, seems to fall with you, darkening, sucked of life. I have to go around and turn the lights on to bring it back from the dead.

*S*aturday afternoon, coming back from shopping, Juliet asks me: where's Dad? And I say, I don't know, he's never here on weekend afternoons, is he?

Maybe he's having an affair, she says, helping me take the bags out of the car.

I hope not, I say.

She looks at my face and nods.

No, she says. It's not his style.

I don't smell another woman around you. Flings maybe. If you were in love with another woman would you still make love to me like you do?

*M*e, going into your studio drowned in darkness, as you are finishing your workout, asking you: what are you doing tonight, and you saying, as I expected: going out to watch the baseball game (it's the sixth game in the World Series). And me, saying: I might be going out with Lola.

I put my arms around your chest, which is softer than it was a year ago, not as buff. You pull your head and neck away from me, not wanting any closeness. And I say, I know, it's hard right now.

You make a little snorting sound of assent, or maybe of disdain, I can't tell. The room is dark. You like to turn the lights on as late as possible, letting yourself go to the night, hiding in it.

The sadness of dusk is seeping deep into the house. I know I have gone to you because I don't want you to drift too far away.

The sadness I feel tonight. The blues. *Peine d'amour.* Lovelorn.

And Juliet who is so angry at me, aggressive, sick of the whole thing, sick of us, taking refuge with her friends, going out every night of every weekend.

The house, deserted, as if it oozed poison.

And me, tonight, unable to give it life. Deserting it, too.

Maybe we'll all leave, abandoning the apartment behind, letting it die. Maybe the four of us will break up. You on one side, Juliet on another. Me and Lola in yet a third place.

Tonight I want to leave. I can't keep the fires of home burning. The cheerfulness, the warmth. I don't have the heart for it. Tonight I want to jump ship too. Pack up and leave.

I am not as afraid as I was. I don't feel I live every day as I did at first with the sword of Damocles over my head. Because the issue has shifted. It's not about you leaving or staying. It's about learning how to depend on my own self. It's about growing up without you.

I've always been very seductive with you, especially the last couple of years, when I started being afraid to lose you. Dressing up for you, showing myself off to you. Turning you on. I'm not sure how to be in the house, around you, now.

Everything between us has loosened up. I have the sensation of floating, of not being firmly anchored, tightly embraced and looked at. As if your gaze had held me together. And the surprise to discover that I can keep going without that loving gaze, that I feel freer without it. Yes, you were holding a mirror up to me, that's what happens in love affairs, in relationships. I was looking for your approval. And now I have to do without.

You don't seem to look for my approval anymore either. You hadn't even told me you were giving portions of your old novel to your editor to read. Apparently she thinks it could make a big commercial novel and that you should rework it. I'm trying to keep my jealousy in check about her.

It feels as if we've moved into a much bigger house, wide open to the outside world, like this dream I just had in which the FDR Drive ran right through our kitchen and living room. We don't know how much space or how much distance we need. I can see you testing: how much to tell me, how much not to tell me. How much you will share or not share with me. How often you go out at night. How domestic you will be. How friendly toward me. How angry. How much sex you will allow yourself to have with me.

2

*B*ASTARD! SCUMBAG! SLEAZEBALL! LIAR! DOUBLE-TIMER! LOWLIFE! MOTHERFUCKER! TRAITOR! SCUM OF THE EARTH! ASSHOLE!

*S*o it isn't Midlife Crisis: Act II. It's Adultery 101. Or both.

*O*h lover, man of my life, sweet sweet lover, you whom I would have trusted with my life, you in front of whom I gave birth to two baby girls, you my man, not my husband, we never called each other husband and wife, but man and woman, you my man, you who have adored me all these years, you have betrayed me, you have fucked me over, you have screwed me big-time.

 $\mathcal{T}$ hree A.M. Friday morning, the day we are to fly to Florida to visit your parents, the weekend of Halloween, I wake up with the brutal, unshakable conviction that you are having an affair. You know these drawings one finds in kids' entertainment books, with an object cleverly hidden in the picture by a trick of the illustrator: in full view, yet invisible. You stare at the drawing again and again and it looks normal to you, a plain family scene: a father and mother waiting for a train on a crowded platform and two kids playing at their feet. And all of a sudden you blink and here it is, staring at you, unmistakable: the lady's profile tucked into the pleats of the father's overcoat. And once you've seen it you cannot unsee it again.

So I decide to finally face the truth. I get up and check around the house to see if I can find any evidence of your betrayal. And here it is, so easy to find: a bunch of receipts from the summer, including expensive hotels, and a page torn off your appointment book with these words: *UPS/FEDERAL EXPRESS, deliver any packages to X.X. and Y.Y.* (her name, your name) *c/o Z.* I stare at the paper as if it's written in code, hoping the words might mean something else than what they seem, but I don't have a clue how to decode them. There are other receipts in that folder where we keep all our receipts. Another weekend, another hotel, in New Jersey. You had told me you were camping out at night in your sleeping bag.

I put everything away and go back up to our bedroom and you wake up and ask me, angrily, in that tone you use with me right now: what's up?

I sit down on the bed next to you and ask you the classic question (we are back in the bad screenplay, uttering tired clichés): are you having an affair? And you say: what has it got to do with anything? So I ask again: are you having an affair? And you duck a second time. The third time you finally say yes, a wisp of a word, blowing through your clenched teeth. For how long? And you say: for fifteen months. Like you've been counting the days, or maybe you've told someone else before, and the answer hits me right in the gut.

Fifteen months. That was the summer before last, the whole time you were writing your novel, the summer we went to Porquerolles Island in the Mediterranean together, the fall when we were making love all the time, the New Year's Eve party when we flirted with each other all evening and I sat on your lap and we kissed at midnight and you were all over me. But it was also the time when you were coming back at 2 A.M. several times a week, refusing to answer my questions, accusing me of clinging to you, and I had convinced myself it was better not to pressure you.

Is it her, your editor?

Yes, you said. How did you know?

I could tell she wanted you. I could see it in her eyes, in her body. I didn't know she had you already.

Did somebody tell you?

I didn't want to tell you about the receipts, about the page torn off your book. It seemed cheap to me, another cliché, the wife rummaging through her husband's papers looking for evidence. I didn't want to admit that I had played the part.

No, I said. But every time I saw her she was always flirting with you. And one time she left a message on our machine, about your book, and it was so erotically charged it was unbearable, but I told myself it was just flirting, that it was the way she was with everybody. But I felt it the minute I first saw her, a couple of years ago, at that party on Gramercy Park. I dismissed her because I thought she came on so strong, she was a little too obvious. I didn't think you'd go for her. But I should've known better, because I am very seductive too, and you fell for me.

And then the details: it started right after I had left for France, in the summer, a little over a year ago. And it resumed in the fall, after you got laid off from your job, and all through the winter.

Now it made sense to me, why I was terrified that you would sell your novel to her, and why, the night the deal was closed, you went out to celebrate your success with her, and not with me.

So that's why she bought your book, I said.

I meant it as a blow, and you felt it.

Thanks, you said, tersely.

There was a moment of silence.

When did you see her?

Whenever she could, whenever I could.

The tone you used to say those words sounded a little whiny, sorry for yourself and for her, as if you two were victims of society's conventions. *My* victims, so to speak, since I was standing in the way.

When you came back at 2 A.M.?

Yes, not always.

You said you were always roaming the streets to write your book. So in fact you were seeing her?

No, sometimes I was in the streets.

On Sunday, when you would disappear for hours, not coming back after grocery shopping until late in the afternoon?

Yes.

But you made love to me all the time. Did you make love to me after coming back from seeing her?

Yes, sometimes.

Did it turn you on?

No. Not really.

There's no word for this. Devastating is the word commonly used.

I should have known. I knew it maybe, unconsciously. The way your sexuality was different.

I thought you were in denial, you said.

And then you said: I had another affair before.

Once again the stiletto in the heart, delicately going for the deep flesh. Your need to unload, to come clean.

For a couple of months, you went on, while I had the job, during the winter. But nothing for sixteen years before.

Once again, the precise dates, as if you had counted, pondered the significance of these numbers.

It had to mean something about our relationship, you said, that all of a sudden after sixteen years I had two affairs back-to-back, it had to mean there was something wrong, that things were not working out between us.

I don't know, I don't know. Not necessarily. Is it the American point of view? That if people have a great relationship they will stay monogamous for a lifetime?

You remember, I said, in July last year, you told me I was the woman of your life? In that little bar on East Ninth Street. You told me it was great living with me, that it was so unpredictable, that you never got bored once with me, that the sexuality changed all the time and was just as exciting?

Yes, you said.

And you started going out with her a few weeks later?

Yes. It had to happen, you said. When you start having affairs it's the sign that things are wrong in a relationship.

I thought I should lash out on you, unload my rage and my anger, at the very least throw some books against the wall. Make a scene. Destroy some furniture. But I didn't do anything. I told myself I didn't want to make a racket, I didn't want to wake up the girls. The truth is that I was dead inside. You had dropped a bomb. Right on the old wound: the fear of being abandoned, of not being loved, of being left behind.

You got up and made coffee. I took a shower and got dressed. I was going to teach that morning.

When I came downstairs to the kitchen, I felt a cold, implacable rage. I remembered when I had decided to leave my French boyfriend Olivier, with whom I lived before you. How I had faced the breakup. I made myself hard and tough.

I said: I cannot accept that. You are going to have to leave, you know that, right?

And you said: yes.

I still didn't get angry at you straight-out. I wanted to spew out torrents of rage, but I couldn't do it. I felt numb. I thought of not going to Florida. I could wait for you and throw you out when you'd come back on Monday.

I had to leave right away: drop Juliet and Lola off at school and go to Hofstra University.

During the drive to Long Island, I tried to imagine packing a bag with your clothes and leaving it outside our front door. Another cliché scene: the betrayed wife kicking out her philanderer husband.

No way. I can't play that scene.

I never packed your bags in my life. Why would I do it today, of all days?

Some women lacerate the guy's best suits with a razor blade, cut up his boxers to shreds. I visualize pouring bleach all over your Agnès b. shirts. Streaking your Armani and Hugo Boss jackets with Day-Glo paint. I see your black bag lying on the mat outside our door, but I cannot see myself kicking you out. My anger is frozen. I can't believe it's over between us. I will drive back to the city this afternoon and it will have been a bad dream, you will be waiting for me with your arms open. It's not true, you will say to me. I lied to you. There's no one else.

Of course I know it's true. But I can't bear to lose you. Not yet. I am not ready yet.

I call you from Hofstra.

I love you, I say. Maybe we can work it out. I couldn't accept the situation to go on for any length of time, and you will have to make a choice, but maybe I can try to live with it until you make up your mind.

Thanks, you say.

You sound relieved, I can tell in your voice.

Then I say: I'm still going to Florida.

Thanks, you say again. I couldn't have faced my parents on my own. They would terrify me. I need you there.

I backed down from the confrontation and you know it. You've tasted blood and I didn't fight back. You will pull on the string as long as I will let you. We are two animals in the quarry. Morals don't apply in this case. It's going to be a fight to the finish.

———

Is knowing better than not knowing? Is not knowing better than knowing? Which is it? Ignorance is bliss. Knowledge is power. Or is it????

Let me make a case for denial, just for the sake of argumentation. How it lets you pretend that what is there is not there. How it protects the status quo. How it keeps everything in balance, however precarious, for a while anyway. How—for the pretender—it allows life to go on with just a slight adjustment, making room for that place where the dark hole of unacknowledged knowledge festers, temporarily jacketed. Denial: a rejection or refusing to acknowledge. How it allowed me to keep my jealousy from destroying me. How it allowed me to deal with an untenable situation without losing control. How I accommodated myself to it like one accepts a blind spot. How it kept me from collapsing. How we both, unconsciously, milked it for maximum erotic pleasure. How we both tacitly accepted it to protect our relationship. To protect our love, maybe. How we were both accomplices in denial: that which is not spoken doesn't exist.

Of the two of us, you are the most relieved that you don't have to lie anymore. And me now, carrying the burden of knowing. You coming down the stairs, crying, telling me how sorry you are for the pain you have caused me, for your cruelty. On the couch, you telling me that I am again the woman you fell in love with.

My strength came right back, I said.

Yeah, you said, but I am not here anymore.

There was regret in your voice.

We talked about our feelings again, something we are not very good at. I suggested you clean up your office upstairs, carve out some peaceful space to work, temporarily, until you decide what you're doing.

But this morning, the swing of the pendulum. I think I should get out of here, you said, find a studio somewhere or borrow an apartment to sort out my feelings. I would come for breakfast and take Lola to school, come in the afternoon to be with the kids. But don't have any illusions. Things will never be the same again between us.

And me, feeling the rage: if you leave, you leave. It's over.

But I don't tell you that. I'm still holding on to you.

I couldn't sleep after we made love last night, you said. It was a moment of weakness. Sex is like a Band-Aid covering up our problems. I don't think we should do that anymore.

You want to break up our sexual relationship?

Yes. I should move out to sort out what I am going to do.

$\mathcal{I}$f he leaves he will come back, my shrink said.

I don't know.

$\mathcal{I}$ am trying to get a feel for the apartment without you. How it would expand, lighten up maybe, without your tormented presence. Without your face brooding over the *New York Times*. Without your toe fungus medicine on the night table (I wonder how romantic that will be on hers?). Your office, cleared up, emptied out. I could take a roommate, have a built-in babysitter as well as extra cash. The accumulation of eighteen years of living together, fifteen years in this apartment. Your books everywhere. The other day you were looking for a book and talked about the need to alphabetize, it was impossible to find anything. You are still at home here.

There will be a moment of truth, when your back will be against the wall. When you will face the void: when you will tip over to one side or the other. Or when I will make you choose: stay or leave. When I will have to kill my love for you. When I will look at what you've done, how you've destroyed our relationship to the point of no return, and despise you. When I will look at you and decide you're not anymore the same man I fell in love with.

There will come a time when you will pack your bag and walk out. Forever. Or not.

All week I have imagined this scene: you, folding your clothes, dropping them into your black bag on the bed. All week

I have been afraid of coming back home to find you packed, afraid to witness your final steps to the door and the door slamming back on you.

But what if you were afraid of taking the final steps yourself?

I want to live with her, you said.

*O*ur dialogues would fit right into a soap.

*T*his is how you started going out with her, you told me: You invited her to see a play with you, a few days after I had flown to Nice.

It was the end of July. The day after my arrival in France, I went to see my father for the first time in my life. I had never known him. My mother had had an affair with him and got pregnant by accident. They talked about getting married but his family didn't approve because she was older than him, and he was still in medical school. They had split up before I was born. After long and tortuous hesitations, I had finally decided I wanted to face the man who had hovered like a ghost over my life.

I called you to tell you about that encounter. You listened to me for a long time. You were warm, wonderfully supportive. You seemed to understand what that meeting meant for me.

Yet a day or two after that you started going out with her. I keep wondering about the coincidence.

*Y*ou didn't go to the co-op meeting last night, for the election of the board. You told me you were giving me your share of the apartment.

*W*hen I treat you with disdain you back down. Are all relationships power struggles, is there always a bully and a victim? Your cruelty and deceit are devastating.

—

*M*y hurt turned to anger yesterday. You said, coming out of the bathroom, drying yourself: if I leave to sort my feelings out will you expect me to come back? You said: don't have any illusions. Things will never be the same between us.

Why are you repeating that all the time? Are you trying to convince yourself? Are you trying to provoke me into a fight? Do you think I don't hear you?

I hear you, but I don't believe you. Not entirely. Maybe that's why you have to repeat yourself so much. It's only when you leave that I will finally believe you.

*H*OW DARE YOU HOW DARE YOU HOW DARE YOU??? Dump me for another woman. *Me plaquer pour une autre femme.* In French the words sting worse, like the tip of a whiplash.

I am frozen in terror. I sit here and I let you hit me. I had put my life into your hands. I had made myself vulnerable to you. In your last novel you wrote about the narrator's first wife that she didn't fight back. I know you were talking about me. You think I don't know how to fight back. But maybe I can learn. Maybe I can finally let it out. You are very primal. For you it's all about the basic urges: sex, hunger, rage, hate. That's what I love in you. I didn't know you would turn them against me.

—

I went to a party last night and I checked out the guys. I am a little rusty but the moves are coming back. It's like riding a bicycle, you never forget.

*W*ell, neither of us can keep the no-sex promise. Last night was erotic and hot and weird as it is these days, because half of your body freezes in terror and the other half plays into my hands.

*M*y chest burns as if there were hot coals sizzling beneath my rib cage. Not a heartbreak exactly, but an inflammation of the tissues. Every day when I come back home I check the air to know which way the wind is blowing. I have trained myself to not care, to take what comes as it may. I put on my fatigues, my warrior mask, my bullet-proof vest, prepare myself for the blows. I try to keep my cool and function under the bombs. I have chosen to play the situation this way: not from the trenches, because I come and go, but staying put. I am letting our story play itself out without forcing it. As a wounded observer on the one hand, but moving with it too, trying to stay ahead of it.

You have made an attempt to destroy me, to undermine me, to break my spirit. You are trying to intimidate me. Given a chance, you turn into a bully. Are you bluffing about leaving? I couldn't say for sure. You have screwed me and betrayed me and lied to me for more than a year. And you're still trying to threaten me. Enough. I am ready to turn the tables. Screw you. You will not scare me, threaten me, put me down, abuse me anymore. I am not scared any-more.

When I feel that way, my chest opens up and I don't feel the coals burning me up.

*Y*ou're a very attentive father right now: driving your daughters to school, picking them up, spending time with them. Yesterday you took them to a screening of *101 Dalmatians*, then to John's Pizzeria. Sunday you took Lola to a playdate and brought her back.

I am observing your moves: yesterday you started to clean up your office, you threw an old printer away. You had books sent to you about traveling on motorcycle around the world. You received a fax announcing rentals of offices downtown, on Maiden Lane, in a building opening next year.

Sometimes I feel better because I imagine you're not going to leave. And sometimes I feel better simply because I feel strong and self-confident. I cannot always tell one from the other.

Do not fool yourself, you said, threateningly, on Saturday morning before I took Lola to dance class. Things will never be the same between us.

No they won't. How could they? You have dropped a bomb between us. We are staring at it and tiptoeing around it for fear it will explode in our face.

When I cannot resist torturing myself I imagine you telling her you love her, stretched on her bed, naked, your cock standing up. I imagine the two of you making love in Massachusetts by the ocean, or in that hotel in New Jersey where you checked in during the summer—that $273 receipt I found in the receipt folder. A weekend in August, crazy in love, your red motorcycle parked in front of the hotel. I love you, you tell her and she sits on your face and you suck her off, her red hair falling all over her face.

One day, last spring, you held me over you with your hands. Your hips are so narrow, you said to me, as if you were surprised.

Now I know why you told me that: her hips are wider than mine. You were comparing us.

I touch myself and come twenty times in a row in a frenzy of erotic fantasy, dripping wet, obsessed with your bodies arched and entwined in every position, her cunt wide open to your mouth, you with a perpetual hard-on. I imagine the two of you fucking everywhere, in the ocean, on her couch, in our car, in her office, in a public bathroom. There is a wild erotic charge to these images, as if the three of us were making love together. I thought of suggesting it, but I know, for having done it, how destructive it is, unless it is among strangers. I do not indulge too often in these fantasies because their power is crushing. Most of the time I don't think of her at all. I tread the perimeter of my house and of my world, watching my feet and my back.

*S*ex between us, you tell me (meaning me and you) is so powerful it is overwhelming.

*T*here are no moorings in our life, no safety, no visibility, only a few sharply familiar moments coming out of the blue, like when we had dinner with a bunch of people after your reading last Sunday night, and it felt like us, very much, together, for a moment. We walked back home side by side, talking quietly.

I had two dreams last night, one while you were at her place, the other one later, at dawn, after you had come back home.

In the first dream, you and I were lying in a bed together,

reconciled. You were talking about your affair, but in my dream the woman was dark-haired and older. It was so easy to fool you, you were saying. I can't believe how easy it was. I wasn't really bothered by what you said. We were laughing together about what had happened.

In the second dream I was going out with a black-haired guy who was taking me to a radio talk show for an interview about my latest novel. The radio guy was kissing me in the hallway, and during the interview I could hear myself talk about my writing in a witty and self-assured way. Afterward you confronted me about cheating on you. You looked wounded. In both dreams I felt powerful and gratified.

I love another woman, I am in love with another woman.

This is what you say to me, with an edge of anger, each stab dismissing what we have shared for eighteen years, reducing it to ashes.

Another version of what you say is this: there have been two major relationships in my life: my first wife and you. She (meaning her) might be the third one. I don't want to miss out on that. It's rare to fall in love like that. I want to live with her.

Each declaration hurtled like a rocket aimed at my heart.

Each like a red flag you raise every time I try to have a conversation with you, every time I bring up the possibility of working things out.

I wonder why you need to be so cruel. So callous. Why you need to repeat yourself so much. Is it because you cannot deliver the final blow? Because you cannot bring yourself to leave?

Or are you just being honest?

When I left Olivier, my French boyfriend, I wrote him a letter acknowledging the love I had felt for him. Not to soften the blow, but to reassure him that my departure didn't erase what we had lived.

Your cruel blows, delivered while you are not leaving, carry another message. They seem to belong to an arsenal of revenge, of resentment, as if I had failed you and you had found a new way to get back at me.

When you deliver the blows a mask of pain is clamped to your face. Fury and guilt freezing your eyes and your mouth in a permanent scowl.

Is our bond still so strong that you need to hack at it with the chainsaw of your words?

*T*wo days ago I came up to you in the living room and told you: we can't pretend that nothing is happening. If you really mean it about loving your children and your family and your home, you've got to consider working things out with me, either by talking with me or seeing a therapist.

It seemed weird, talking like that, taking the American way: consulting a therapist to try to fix our relationship. I never thought I would throw our life into the jaws of a counselor. It's like calling a priest to bring the last sacraments, *l'extrême-onction*, to the patient when you hear the death rattle.

We talked for four and a half hours on the couch, smoking cigarettes, till night came and it was time to go pick up Lola. We talked about us (again: something we never really did when we were still "alive"), and what went wrong for you, things you have not entirely forgiven me for: the abortion I had ten years ago, my failure to help you pull together that long novel you had worked on for years, my own struggles as a writer, my lack of acknowledgment of you (you think I saw you as a loser), your inability to feel at ease in the French culture, particularly in my middle-class, uppity family. Each issue so loaded it could have brought any couple to its knees in just a few years. I told you your expectations were so high that it was hard to always meet them, and I asked you if your love was conditional to my accomplishments. And you said no, you fell in love with me when I hadn't accomplished that much.

And then you talked about her.

You said she comes from the same background as you— working-class or lower-middle-class, immigrant family; that she makes you feel like an important novelist, and that when you sold your book you thought you had turned into a new person, that your dark sides were gone. And now you weren't so sure anymore. I said I felt the same at the time of my first American novel, that for a while I thought I was cured of all my anxieties.

Last night, when I was putting Lola to bed, she said: we are not acting like a family. What's wrong, Mom? I was panicked during the afternoon, she went on. I thought my heart was breaking.

This morning in bed, you had your back to me, your legs curled into mine, I was massaging the back of your head.

I love you, I said. I know you could be happy again with us, that we could have an exciting relationship again.

Your whole body stiffened. This is not what you want to hear.

I have noticed you treat me better when I come and go and don't pay too much attention to you, when I don't show you my fear of losing you.

You've been here nonstop for the last five days, eating here, cooking with me, taking care of the kids. This afternoon you told me you had made an appointment with a shrink. You seemed relieved, your shoulders looser and a softness in your face. You fell asleep on the couch reading a motorcycle journal, evading in a vicarious trip. Afterward we cooked dinner together and I was almost happy, eating the hamburgers you had broiled and the potatoes I had sautéed (no more swiss chard, no more broccoli, no more health food, I have canceled the box of organic vegetables; our cooking has been reduced to the lowest common denominator), while watching "Friends" on TV, the familiar intimacy and well-being almost palpable between us.

Gore Vidal said: art doesn't imitate life, life imitates cheap TV.

In a movie, there would be a gun. I would shoot you, or her, or both of you in a fit of passion. Or you would plot my demise with her, coldly, to make it look like an accident—poison or tinkering with the car brakes—and after the funeral you would wait a decent amount of time and then have her move into our house, so that you would have everything you want: your home, your kids, and your new woman. I am the one who stands in the path of your happiness. And then Juliet might run away from home, or get involved in hard drugs. Or she might shoot her. In another version of the teleplay, you two would live happily ever after, and have children together who would become Lola's best friends. Another version yet would have you wrestle with your dilemma and conflicting loyalties and love, and decide to break up with her and reconcile with me.

Or I would shoot her through the heart.

Soon it will be three months that I have been back from France. I have decided to settle in the crisis. I try to find ways to cope, to find small moments of peace, to laugh at the situation, to take some distance.

I need a man in my life. A man to love, a man to hold in my arms, a man to take inside of me, a man to make me wet, a man to make me scream and make me come, come, come. You have been that man. The man I could say everything to. The man who adored me. The man who touched my soul. Were you a delusion? I thought we were soul mates forever.

I thought the edge was far, you said. And suddenly I was right at the edge.

I didn't even see any edge. You were my man and I trusted you. Was I wearing a blindfold?

You, who can be so charming and sweet and funny, have turned against me like a snake. Your face, fist-tight, deep furrows between your eyes. Stormy forehead. Your shoulders, rounded around your chest. Trapped into your rage.

Did you really fall out of love with me?

You never said: I'm unhappy with you. You were annoyed, angry, frustrated. You were running out of the house. Coming back late, going to bars, clubs, hanging out. Suddenly, overnight, you turned into another man. But you kept saying: I love you, I want you. You are the woman of my life. I've never been bored one minute with you. I love my life with you. You never stopped making love to me. You said you loved my breasts, you loved my cunt. You had your hand between my legs in public places. Why do you resist me now: are you afraid to betray her?

Our last year together has been contaminated. When I look back and remember moments, they have turned radioactive: when you fingered me in the car on our way to eat bouillabaisse in Saint-Tropez, you had already slept with her. When you gave me black lacy lingerie last Christmas and pulled my nipples out of the bra cups and told me how much you liked my tits, you were already falling in love with her. When you met her for a drink the day you sold your book and didn't come back until 2 A.M., you had fucked her. You always came back home between 2 A.M. and 2:30 A.M., like clockwork, you never came back later than that. I told myself you were hanging out with friends in a bar after business dinners, so many bars I tried to imagine; or maybe that there were women, but nothing serious, nothing that would threaten our relationship. You said you liked to hang out and roam the streets of New York late into the night, and I believed you; you said you used to do that in your twenties, that it was something you really liked to do.

When you made love to me at 2 A.M., had you even washed your dick, or did you dip it straight into my cunt? To be honest, a lot of the time during the spring you couldn't actually fuck me. I was concerned about that. Now I can see why. It was hard to service two women back-to-back, wasn't it? You wanted me to get you off while you kept your arm folded over your chest and closed your eyes, your forehead tense in concentration. Were you thinking of her? Were you thinking of me when you made love to her?

$\mathcal{I}$s this journal an epitaph to our love affair?

$\mathcal{W}$hen we came back from France the summer before last, you decided to grow dreadlocks. You let the top of your hair grow and took to twisting little strands of it between your fingers to get the dreads started. It freaked me out. Not because I don't like dreads, but because the idea seemed to have come from the outside, sprouted overnight, so to speak. It was a new persona you were developing, and you were throwing it in my face: take that, bitch, see if you can stop me. See how cool I am. See how bad I am. I started to call you coolman. Hey, coolman, I'd say to you, when I thought your attitude was too much. Each time you

twisted a strand of hair I felt stabbed and betrayed. Eventually
you dropped the dreads, and you had a Persian lamb hat with
flaps handmade by your hat maker for the winter. That same
Persian lamb hat she put on her head at that publishing party we
all went to last Christmas, playing with it and with you, and
finally bringing it to me as if the hat belonged to me by way of
you. I saw the game, but I convinced myself it was flirtation, and
that it was harmless.

Every day the betrayal seems deeper, every day the gap
widens. Every day I feel the loss a little more.

―――――

There are days when I cling to you and days when I let you go,
and the days when I let you go, it's as if you had died. The
house—the flowers on the piano, the couch, the magazines on
the coffee table—is drained of life. Gray, limp, wilted. There are
days when I feel the loss like a sudden drainage of energy and
the aloneness is primal, inevitable. There are days now when
what we have lived together seems to belong in the past, irretrievable, a passion that happened, a passion that was.

I can accept that you're having an affair, but not the idea that
you might not love me anymore.

Yesterday, looking for a pair of gloves, I touched the tattered
scarf, tie-dyed in shades of gray and green, that you were wearing with a tweed jacket when you met me at the airport in LA,
when I went to visit you after our first night in New York. You
were still wearing it, hanging loose from your neck, when you
lay down on your bed and offered yourself to me, hands
stretched over your head, legs slightly apart. I had never seen a
man offer himself like that, almost like a woman. You trusted me,

already. You knew you could be yourself with me, you knew that I was yours. Our sexuality runs from male to female, and we both can play both parts. The scarf still smells of you, the smell of first passion.

I can see that sometimes, when I write about our relationship, I use the present tense, and sometimes I use the past. And I don't know if I should start mourning it or hoping for it to come back to life.

Maybe I need time to lose you, bit by bit, peel your soul off me.

I wonder if for you it's all gone, if our passion is reduced to some distant memories that have already turned stale. Fading, unrecognizable. I can see that you are forgetting the details, that you have already moved on. I am left holding our love like the end of a sheet that nobody will help me fold.

Each time I turn from you in anger, like last night when I slept in the guest bedroom because you had gone out to see her, I am losing you a little.

I wish I didn't have to see you. We lay down at night together, your body curled into mine, my arms around your chest, or your arms around mine, caressing my breasts, and I smell your underarms and I know if I stretch my hand your cock will swell between my fingers like it always does, and I wonder if our bodies will ever stop wanting each other. But you resist me as if I were the devil, a dark power that wishes your downfall.

———

Today I detached myself from you. I became whole again. You went out tonight, a dinner with the editor-in-chief of a men's magazine, and the three of us—Juliet, Lola and I—stayed home and hung out freely, eating Cuban rice and beans that you don't like, and making a mess on the big couch, in the middle of thrown pillows and comforters.

I try to imagine you at some of these dinner or cocktail parties, playing the part of the rebel writer: the wild hair, the leather jacket, the motorcycle helmet, the twin turquoise studs in your right ear, the oversize clothes, everything carefully put together with the kind of care that models lavish on themselves—you are a great guy to go shopping with, you're really into clothes, for men and for women. I imagine the two of you at these parties, the hot couple on the rise. I imagine the two of you talking about your plans of success after sex: when you are recognized as the baddest badass novelist in America, when she's the most powerful fiction editor in town. The Maxwell Perkins and Ernest Hemingway of the nineties.

Sorry for the sarcasm.

It's easier for me to believe you're leaving me out of devouring ambition rather than out of love for another woman.

When you are in the house these days, it's as if you were burning a hole through the ceiling and the floor. Your torment trails around you, killing all joy and lightness. You lie down on the bed or hunch over your computer checking your e-mail, or whisper on the phone for hours, surrounded by a barbed-wire fence and a huge NO TRESPASSING sign written in blood.

Before you left, tonight, you held Lola in your arms while she was watching "Buzz" on TV and you asked Juliet, who has a cold, if she wanted chicken soup—the broth you prepared for her last night. It was you at your most tender, your most loving.

But tonight I didn't let my feelings of tenderness for the kind of man, of father that you can be, weaken me to the point of despair. Tonight I looked at you, the man I have loved more than any other person in my life, more than my mother, more than the father I never had, and I wanted to take you in my arms and lean my head against your shoulder, but I didn't. Tonight I am detached from you and I just looked. I saw the softness in your smile when Lola made a silly comment, I saw the smile I love, but I didn't melt into a heap of longing and desire. And when you kissed the girls good-bye and only said good-bye to me from a distance, to show me that you loved them but not me, not like that, not like a man loves a woman, not like you used to love me, I didn't shudder. I said good-bye and set the containers of rice and beans on the coffee table for our dinner and proceeded to eat heartily.

During the night I dreamed of my ex-boyfriend and you. Olivier, who used to drive a burgundy-red Yamaha XS 1200, was coming back from a motorcycle trip, wearing a strange pair of chaps in fur or fake-fur over his bike pants to keep him warm. Then you showed up in your own motorcycle outfit, and Olivier told you how warm his chaps were, that you should try on a pair. Are you two becoming one: ur-biker-man destined to disappear from my life? But the dream was friendly, there was no betrayal, on the contrary: you two were coming to me, not pulling away. And you were coming home.

I asked you if you are using condoms with her and you said no. I asked you if she was HIV-negative and you said yes. I asked if you had both been tested since you started making love with her and you said no, that you trusted her. I asked you: are you sure she hasn't been sleeping with other guys, and you said yes.

I couldn't stand the conversation and you couldn't stand it either, and yet I couldn't let it go. You became increasingly angry and muttered, without conviction: maybe I should leave. And I said, quickly, no, no, it's not that, but when you have several partners, you need to think about these things. You walked out of my room, back up to your office.

After a little while, I went upstairs to talk to you and I said: how can you be so hostile to me, you treat me as if I was a stone standing in your path that you want to kick out of the way. You've loved me and adored me all these years, why don't you take me in your arms and say, I'm so sorry. Do you realize how hard it is for me?

I don't know why I was going on that way. I felt so foolish with my pain dangling in front of me. You were doodling on a yellow Post-it pad, one of those cartoons you do, large funny face with tiny body, and didn't say anything. Later, when I went upstairs to the bathroom, you were lying on the bed reading, your face a tight-fisted mask of anger and pain.

We blew it, baby. How can we have blown it like that? What subterranean forces undermined us?

I notice that you say: maybe I should leave, but never: I should break up with her. I also notice that you don't leave.

We've been so happy here, we've made love everywhere, on the couch, on the kitchen counter, on the floor, in the shower, on the bed, so often. Not so long ago you asked me, what is the longest time we've stayed without making love? And we figured it was probably less than a week. When we went to see *Once Were Warriors*, the New Zealand movie, we talked about the sexual relationship between the husband and wife, even though they had grown-up children. How vibrant their sexuality was, in spite of his violence, in spite of the fact that he was abusing her. I don't know why the movie struck such a chord in us. After all, you are not abusing me, but you recognized the violence in these warrior men, so proud, so frustrated, with no outlet for their manhood other than drinking and taking power over their women. We talked about how ambiguous the volatile combination of sexuality and violence was, but you liked that they were so sexual together after all those years, like we were.

And now you say: sexuality is not all there is to a relationship, as if I was a slut you had picked up on the street, and not your writing and editing partner, the woman who's shared every aspect of your life, and the mother of your children.

I felt suffocated, you say. I wanted something else.

If I looked for an affair, you say, that means there had to be something wrong with our relationship.

I think your feelings are more complicated and conflicted than you let on.

All these feelings hidden under the mask of the perfect husband and father, all these feelings pent-up inside of you for years, festering under the *I love you* and the *I love my life with you* and *everything will be okay*, now bursting forth with a vengeance.

There was something irresistible pushing you forward, as if you had climbed into a spaceship racing at 2000 miles per hour and you had no control over it. I saw you take off and I felt the speed of air and I hung on to your rocket by my fingernails, afraid to lose you. You were spinning out of control, and I was just standing by, hoping you would run out of gas, come back to earth. Earth meaning me. Meaning what we had made together.

Fragile human construction: a family based on sexual passion, two beautiful girls, two writing careers, two different cultures, two different social classes. Everything resting on our unstable shoulders. That was the beauty of it. We always said how wacko it was, how we were just winging it. How it worked, magically. And how we managed to have remained very much alive and vibrant together.

You said I fell apart all the time, but you are turning out to be the one who couldn't handle it anymore.

People say how solid and strong and reliable you are.

I, of all people, should have known better. How you are also made of quicksand and deceptive, murky waters.

We were not solid, we were a construction made of love and vulnerability. And a breath of wind, a moment of recklessness when you said to yourself, I don't care, I don't give a damn, is blowing it away.

The other day you told me: I didn't mean to fuck up my life. I don't know what happened. I have no idea how I find myself where I am now. As if you had lost control and had landed on another shore and you couldn't, or wouldn't, come back.

Sometimes I wish you had crashed on your motorcycle and died.

They say people have an affair because they are not getting what they want at home. They don't really mean to break up, it's a way of letting the other person know—unconsciously—that something's wrong. And now you are stuck. You are torn, you are tormented. You stay awake at night, your arms rigidly clamped to your face. You are in love, you are deeply involved, you have fantasized another life. But we are still in this life together, running the daily show of domesticity. Tonight you did the hamburgers and I did the broccoli and the salad, and you put Lola to bed, as you do almost every night that you are here.

Our new routine is dinner at the round coffee table, kneeling on pillows, the TV turned on to daily reruns of "Blossom" and "Fresh Prince of Bel Air," followed by occasional fresh episodes of "90210" or "Friends" or "Seinfeld." We watch avidly and laugh at the jokes. If we are in the mood for a conversation we toss it on top of the TV dialogues, there's less pressure in case it doesn't fly. It's a relief for all of us. We never could handle the dinner episodes at the kitchen table when, invariably, somebody would lose their temper within five minutes (usually you) and somebody would leave the table in a funk (you or Juliet) and never come back.

Our best time was making love after the kids were asleep or in the afternoon, or working together. I don't know if you would do better at the dinner table with another woman and two kids.

*Y*ou love me. You love me not.

*H*ow can you not love me anymore? I don't believe you don't. All my feelings are shut down, you say. I don't know what I'm feeling.

This is what *I* feel: rage and tenderness and sexual passion and contempt and disgust and disappointment and eternal love and despair and desire and overwhelming pain and humiliation. I feel a rainbow of emotions, the full range, a whole orchestra of them, from violins to bass to the rhythm section. All of it at the same time, a jazz section gone berserk, deafening. And you don't feel anything? Your eyes are dead. In bed, at night, with no lights on, you open your legs secretly to me, you push yourself between my thighs, you drip and swell into my hands, you play with me. We lose breath into each other's mouth. There's a pulse between us, primal. Our bodies want each other. We'll always be lovers, don't you know, I whisper to you and stretch into your arms.

You stay mute.

I can't believe that you don't love me anymore.

But that's not what you say. I love you, you say. But I fell in love with her.

On the drive back from Hofstra University I dissect the difference between *to love* and *to be in love*.

One day you make love with her, the next day with me.

Some days I think I could live like that: share you with her. Other days the rage suffocates me: you must laugh with her, smile that smile that makes her moan, your head a little cocked to the side, shoulders leaning back against a wall, body offered. You don't take women. You offer yourself to them. It is the power of your seduction that you allow yourself to be wanted, that you don't feel threatened by women's desire, that you don't need to conquer, you'd rather be gloriously passive. You like women to take over. That's how you got me, by letting me take the lead. Take me, you said to me, take care of me, I will follow you anywhere. You made me feel like the most adventurous lover, the sexiest woman alive. You, the teenager forever dazzled by women's treasures.

Now she is the one dazzling you. You let her come to you and take you in her arms. I love you, you tell her. I am in love with you. I want to be with you. I want to live with you. You twist her long hair between your fingers, you twist it in a knot. You look her in the eyes, your eyes melt into hers, the way lovers' do.

But you already love me. You already want me. You already live with me.

You said I was the woman of your life.

You said that to me in that little bar on East Ninth Street, your legs entwined with my legs, a glass of scotch in your hand. It was a little over a year ago. You are the man of my life, I told you, and we kissed passionately.

Remember?

And now you don't know anymore. She might be the next woman of my life, you say.

How can you?

You love me. You love me not.

Your ass in my hand. Your balls, hardening under my fingers. But you don't look me in the eyes. We grope at each other in the dark, breathless. Secretly. As if our love was the shameful one, the one you had to hide.

───────

*Y*our hair, a halo of curls around your head, spilling over your forehead, the sharp angle of your jaw and your trademark round glasses, your ripped jean shirt hanging open over your T-shirt, your whole look carefully disarrayed, just so. You have been invited to read fifteen minutes of *Lolita* in that twelve-hour marathon reading of Nabokov. Sarcastic, funny, passionate, you read as if it were your own work, sneaking behind the words, and delivering a decidedly un-Nabokovian performance.

I should be hating you and I don't. Not at this moment. The rage will come back, I know, another time. Carrying swelling and seething images of betrayal. But not now. Here, at the podium, you have stepped back from my grasp, painfully removed. I find you achingly beautiful, self-assured. You've finally come into your own. Now is the dull pain of seeing you, who have been mine, as a separate, intimate stranger.

When did I lose you? What day, what instant? Was it a gradual, slow frittering away of our love, or did it happen from the inside out, the conflicts pushing their underground way like termites until our relationship exploded, rotten from the core?

You didn't come to me after your reading, as you would have done before, you walked straight outside, and I found you talking with two people on the sidewalk. Not unfriendly but distant. Insisting, in public places, to show that we are not together. And yet later on, we sat side by side—but not too close—and talked on the steps of the gallery.

I am, I see, in the process of recording the subtle moves and scales of emotion blowing between us, as if we were improvising a piece of music together and I was marking down the notations.

Distance. Physical and emotional. A huge gap when you come back from seeing her. A cement wall when you read the newspaper in the morning and refuse to say a word. A smaller gap when we talked about the greenmarket and Christmas this morning, natural, relaxed, going about the business of being a family, this complex and deeply interconnected tissue of emotions and routines.

And now the distance that I am putting between myself and you, staying detached for fear of being pulled back and not being able to trust it, afraid of getting severely burned again.

The desire not to talk about this for a while. To let it sit. To live it without screaming, without running away. Letting the fear and the grief and the tenderness flow in and out of me. Watching it happen at a slight remove . . . Until tomorrow when I will grab every painful image that comes my way and pounce on every excruciating emotion and rub myself raw until I can barely breathe.

*T*oday, Saturday, you spent the whole day with us. I don't think you had spent a whole Saturday at home for months. You cooked scrambled eggs with onions and cheddar cheese and bacon. Tonight we are going out to a birthday party together. Today you were here, not somewhere else. Today at home the wall was paper-thin. But I don't know what it means, only that there is less tension and I can relax a little.

I went through a period when I consulted the I Ching several times a day to find out if I was handling the situation the best way I could, and if the outcome was positive, according to my desires. I thought of seeing an astrologer I had consulted years ago when I was having a real bad time. But she's expensive, and I don't want to spend any money right now. The I Ching will have to do. I did it again this week, once. But the question was too blunt, I think.

I asked the I Ching if you still loved me. The answer had something to do with measurements and a bamboo stick. I don't know how to measure your love counting the joints on a bamboo stick. The I Ching is a better guide when the questions are about strategy, what to do rather than what is, maybe because it was originally devised as an oracle for Chinese generals. And then it always tells you to be correct in your heart, to be sincere. But the three of us, I presume, are sincere, and yet we desire different outcomes of the situation.

This is the advice people are giving me: get rid of him already, pull yourself together, take care of yourself, prepare for all eventualities, see a lawyer, be sweet as pie with him, be patient, take a lover, it'll blow over, no Jewish man leaves his wife and children, put up with it for a while, stand up to him, he needs a good fight, don't make love with him, play hard to get, ignore him, it's okay to make love, mind your own business, be a charming wife, talk to her, tell her to back off, lay off your man, don't do anything, relax, get angry, scratch his eyes out, don't give him too much time, everybody will know you're a cuckold, give him enough time, you may need to wait until the spring, wait until she makes a mistake, don't put any pressure on him, put your foot down, put his back against the wall, see how long you can tolerate the situation, protect your interests, think of the children, make sure you get the apartment, you're going to be sick of it soon, if it goes on too long, you're the one who's not going to want to take him back, tell him to fuck off, don't say anything, let it ride for a while. And so on . . .

I talk too much on the phone to too many people. It's like digging into the wound and pressing on the pus. It relieves me for a while and then the pain comes back.

———

$\mathcal{O}$ur relationship wide open, hooked to monitors. Is it still breathing? Taking the pulse. Weak but steady. Vital signs: shut-down.

————————

$\mathcal{I}$ took the offensive last night, at the birthday party. We were sitting side by side on a couch, talking about us.

I'm out the door, you said to me. If I had money I'd be gone. At least, that's what I say to myself. But I am broke.

You don't want to leave, I told you. It's like you're split in two: one here, one there.

It's true, you said.

If you're here, it's because you want to be. If you've got to go, go. Nobody's holding you back. You don't have a ball and chain around your ankle. The door's open.

You laughed and you said: you're using the same psychology with me as with your daughter.

I laughed too.

You told me once I was the smartest woman you've ever been with, I said. You acted out of rebellion, you wanted to break all the rules, act without constraint. But you're playing with fire and you're going to get burned. I should have con-fronted you a year ago, but I felt too insecure, too weak in the relationship. Plus, I didn't understand the signs, maybe for cul-tural reasons. American men, I don't know. Or maybe it's you. I didn't get it. You had been completely opaque. Maybe you don't read me very well either, for the same reason. But you had a field day with me. You thought I would put up with everything. You forgot who I am.

Later, as we were walking back home, I told you: I am crazy about you, I wouldn't bother otherwise, I know what we have together. But I am not elastic forever. You're going to lose me and I am irreplaceable.

I know, you said.

And when we came back home I told you: you know what I really resent? It's that you put up a wall between us because you're so scared to get involved with me again. If you're going to be wild, be wild all the way, you've been betraying me for more than a year, you can betray her too. I came first, I am the one you're committed to.

You laughed.

In bed you finally knocked down the wall and took me in your arms. We stayed in each other's arms, me lying on top of you, for a long time, and I felt the pulse between us, this big wave that rocks us and swells every time we touch each other. What's between us, I asked you, is it sex? No, you said, it's 95 percent emotion, 5 percent sex. I laughed: plus we know how to do it. You laughed too. I had my mouth on your mouth. Our bodies were riding the crest, but we didn't make love right away. We talked for a long time. I hadn't felt so close to you for a long time. I felt your hair, how wiry it is, I ran my hand through its fur. We made love again in the morning.

But when I came back from dropping off Lola at a playdate, you were gone. It upset me for a little while, then I thought you had to run to her to reassure yourself that you were still with her.

So I went shopping, bought sexy clothes, spent your money and had fun while you did what the fuck you wanted to do. And I felt vibrant, in the street, the energy running through me and connecting me to the world.

I thought of that woman I had met at a friend's house, one day. She was telling me about her husband's affair and how, when she found out, she had never felt more alive in her life.

Maybe it's true, what they say, that an affair can save a marriage. If it doesn't destroy it. Make it or break it.

You have more to lose than me. I should be the jilted lover, the abandoned wife, begging you to stay, but I feel more alive than ever. Suddenly I am the one telling you: I'm going to run out of patience and you're going to lose everything.

Three pages a day, that's my rhythm. I am like a slug leaving a trail of gook behind me: let it be known that I have walked that path. There will be no medals for this melodramatic, tragicomic, heart-wrenching, backbreaking, desolately banal episode, but a few literary—or something—droppings.

I had told my mother not to come for Christmas. I thought her presence would complicate things. Maybe it was cowardice, fear of asserting myself in front of you: this is the way I am doing Christmas, whether you like it or not. But Juliet and Lola ganged up on me and said we couldn't have Nanny buy presents and not invite her, that it was the Christmas tradition and it wouldn't be Christmas without her. I agreed: if you want to fuck up your life, I don't have to let you fuck up mine. I had already decided to have the Christmas Eve dinner, a tradition, too, for the last three years. So Christmas will be our usual Christmas. The show must go on. *Le Roi est mort. Vive le Roi.*

Well, the king is not entirely dead. The vital signs are steady, if barely perceptible.

I'm out the door, you said. If I had the money . . . (I am not letting myself be insulted). Yeah, you've got your exit route mapped out. We'll see today: you're expecting news from LA, an idea you pitched to your agent that could make a big commercial movie. The agent has gotten bids from several major studios. The idea, by itself, would bring you a lot of money.

I am not holding you back. If you want to go, go. Take the money and run, baby.

You didn't get any phone call from LA.

You're clean-shaven again. I didn't notice it right away. I usually notice everything about you.

It's been two weeks, you tell me, I was looking grubby and gray.

Your beard is getting gray, it gives your age away. I understand: I henna my hair every three weeks, make sure the gray is covered. I loved your three-day beard. I thought it was so sexy. But it's not me you want to please these days.

3

The relationship between us as we know it is over.

These are the words you use in front of the shrink (shrimp, I insist on calling him in my head).

Did you hear what he said, the guy asks. I say yes. And how does that make you feel, the shrimp insists, playing his fucking part. Go ahead, emote.

So I give it to them.

Devastated. That's how I feel. You're my life, my love, my home. You've been the love of my life, as I have been the woman of your life.

I put my face into my hands and don't look at you two for a while.

Is that what you wanted to hear?

It's as if the words we say to each other in the presence of the shrimp have more weight, more significance than when we talk to each other on our own. They hang in the air and ripple for a long time. They have a solemnity about them, as if we were exchanging sacraments in front of a priest. Breakup words instead of taking the vows.

I want to move on, you say. You're too needy. She doesn't need me. There's no pressure with her.

When we came back home you said: it was painful to see that we were in the same room, but not on the same page.

That's the damage you did by keeping your other life hidden from me. On the phone my mother said: he's trying to make you catch up with him. It's over, he says. Accept it. Then see what happens.

You didn't get any phone call from LA today either. Too late in the year, the studios are saying. No money left in the budgets. You press forward, pull some strings. I can feel your tension mounting.

This morning, Thanksgiving morning, I wake up from a deep sleep thinking the time is coming to let you go.

I do the I Ching, throw my three copper pennies six times. I get Chung Fu, 61: Inmost Sincerity. "The superior man, in accordance with this, deliberates about cases of litigation and delays the infliction of death." Which I translate as: I should go back to the shrimp for more sessions and wait a little longer to give you the boot.

On the phone a friend tells me you said she was glamorous.

A new window opens for me: you, insecure little boy, are dazzled by her clothes, her connections, her self-sufficiency.

What about me, am I not glamorous too?

Haven't I got my share of Issey Miyake, Agnès b., Romeo Gigli, Azzedine Alaïa and Jean-Paul Gaultier, most of them secondhand or hand-me-down, granted, but still!

The shrimp, trying to hear you: so the sex is a place where you two can go easily, and it's powerful and everything feels right, it's a primitive place, but it's a fantasy too, and in the morning it doesn't correspond to reality? Does it feel like a lie?

Yes, in a way, you say.

I don't want to have my relationship with you dissected by the shrimps. We are not on the operating table anymore. This is the morgue. But the corpse is still warm. Maybe the patient is still alive.

So I am overly needy, and I make you think of your mother, depending on you emotionally, and the sex may be a lie, and you're telling me: it would be more honest if you cried, rather than this bravado, but if I cry I make you think of your mother and you are terrified of my neediness.

You've got me tied up into knots. You're trying to destroy my self-confidence. You're trying to destroy your image of me. In French they say: when you want to shoot your dog you say it's mangy. But let me tell you: you can get me down, but you can't kill me.

When we came back from the shrimp I said: it felt as if you were shooting me in the back.

That got you mad.

Meanwhile, your other fantasy, the other, glamorous, wonderful, happy life that awaits you just on the other side of the wall, is growing more and more appealing as our relationship looks to you sicker and more terrifying, and your anger at me grows, and your need to shut me off, to utter definitive words, to end it, grows.

Baby, I think it's time for you to go.

Enough. I say, enough.

Go, do not torture me anymore. Do not destroy us anymore.

Can't you have the elegance to leave without destroying what you've built?

Go and face yourself. See what you are really about. See if you are living your life out of fear or out of strength. See if you've got the balls, or just the accoutrements, the posture of a man: the leather jacket, the motorcycle, the swagger, the curses.

I am curious: I want to know who the man I've loved is, what he is truly about.

The house pitches in the storm, a ship tossed about the waves. The TV is on all the time, soothing the girls to oblivion, "The Jenny Jones Show," "The Ricki Lake Show," "The Sally Jessy Raphael Show," "Buzz," "Blossom," "Fresh Prince of Bel Air," "Beverly Hills 90210," "Friends," "Single Guy," "Mad About You," "Seinfeld," "X-Files," the continuous loop of American pop culture as background for our breakup.

Are you running away from me or from your own demons? You look at me as if I owned them, as if I were responsible for them, since with her you feel like a new man, fearless.

Look at the new, improved you, I said one day at a book party, in front of several people, pulling your taupe fedora down over your eyes. I was trying to make the gesture playful but we both knew how aggressive it was.

You glowered at me and wouldn't speak to me for the rest of the evening.

I think I would have loved you without your insecurities. I would have loved the man you are turning out to be—powerful, confident, worldly—if you hadn't rejected me in order to be that man.

But we'll never know that, will we? There's also the issue of my competitiveness, of my ego, the possibility that I might be jealous of your success.

It may take months—weeks anyway—until you get any substantial money, I don't know how much you think you need to make your move. But I don't think I am going to wait that long.

I relish the idea of pushing you out penniless, without any option other than moving in with her and setting your computer on the corner of a desk. See how cool it looks, coolman. See how glamorous, see how sexy. See how it feels to have no room of your own and no turf, and no money to share the rent. See how it feels to have cut yourself off from the home you have constructed with your own hands, and from your family.

Is it just another classic American story of reinventing yourself? You already did it once with me. One new woman for each new phase of your life. How neat. How exciting. Brave new fucking world.

If you've got to do it, do it.

Go for the kill, go for the jugular.

But you can't, can you? You're waiting for me to give you the boot, aren't you?

*O*ur relationship is over, you said in front of the shrimp yesterday.

But you didn't exactly say that. You said, weirdly: our relationship as we know it is over.

As we know it?

Did you hear what he said? asked the shrimp.

Yes.

How does it make you feel?

I took a breath. I didn't look at either of you.

Devastated. That's how it makes me feel. He is the man of my life, my love, the man I have built a life with, I said to the shrimp. You've been my man, and I've been your woman, I said to you.

I couldn't look at you. I closed my eyes and put my hands over my face. I didn't cry. It was like a moment in church. *Recueillement*, we say in French. I held the pain for a while inside of me. It was private. I didn't want you or the shrimp to see it.

You didn't want to take that editing job, remember? I pushed you to take it. And then you realized that the world loved you and I was the one holding you back. Do I need to push you again?

*S*ections of the *New York Times* are strewn about the kitchen table, copies of *The New Yorker*, *New York*, *Esquire*, *Wired*, *Rolling Stone* cover the sunny yellow-enamel surface. The loose galleys of your novel are piled in one corner, with your Mont Blanc pen carefully placed on top. And you, holding on to your usual place, stake your turf sullenly as if to defy me, as if you still had a right to it.

No sun today. A gray Thanksgiving day. No thanks to give to anyone on my part.

*A*t Thanksgiving dinner there was a magazine editor we're friends with, who—innocently—lathered praise over her: how great she is, what a great editor, how beautiful.

The three of us were sitting around a coffee table. You on the couch, the editor and I across from you. You were nodding, perhaps sadistically or naively thrilled that I was hearing these praises. The words hit me like small, deadly pellets, shot one at a time. "Beautiful" hung in the air for a while. I watched you, frozen, trying to gauge if you were proud of your lover or embarrassed for me. Maybe both. Your face didn't give anything away. What a poker face you can have, you who has such a sensitive face at other times, how clever you are at not showing your hand, which is probably the reason you deceived me so well and for so long.

But this morning my rage was nearly uncontrollable. And yet again, I didn't let it out. I was about to ask you to leave. I spent half the day on the phone with friends, to talk myself out of it.

Time is on my side.

We need time.

I need time anyway.

––––––––

*W*hy you are still here and why I did not throw you out are questions that I don't really know how to answer.

I am hearing rumors: you said that her apartment was too plush to bring the kids to it. You said you were in love with her. You said you loved us both.

Sometimes I want to hear the rumors in order to try to gauge your mood, your intentions of the day, of the week. In order to decide what to do, if I should wait another week, another day. Other times I want to plug my ears and not talk to anybody anymore.

*W*hen you came back from her place Lola asked you: were you at your girlfriend's, Dad? The way kids do these things: drop a bomb with a smile.

You tried to laugh it off: where did she get that from? I told you it was not funny. You turned against me: who told her that? I said I didn't and that it was in the air and that Lola had picked it up somehow. Your anger was mounting, as it does every time you are pinned down.

Lola asked a second time: did you go to your girlfriend's? You didn't say anything. I said: you've got to take responsibility. You glowered at me: who's not taking responsibility?

I was going through the mail that you had just brought up, and my hands started to shake with rage. I didn't want to fight about that. I am scared to confront you, scared of your anger, scared to blow off my chances forever with you. I changed the subject. By the way, I said, as long as you live here, I think you shouldn't talk to too many people about what's going on, to protect me, I'm asking you to be sensitive about it, because I am the one who's exposed and humiliated. I'm hearing things, I'm hearing rumors, I can't control the rumors, but I am asking you not to talk about it.

Surprisingly you heard me and your anger dropped. Maybe it was my voice that touched you. Maybe you felt my vulnerability. But it's tricky for me to show it to you, because I don't want to beg, I want to keep my dignity (or what's left of it). But don't you believe for a second that I am going through this as if it were a breeze.

I cherish too much what we've had, I said. I don't want it to be destroyed. I love you too much, or I've loved you too much, to let what we have be— I don't know what word I used exactly, something that meant trampled, or destroyed.

And then, because I was going to have dinner tonight with common friends, I told you I wasn't trying to separate you from our friends, that I didn't expect them to take sides, that I didn't mean to cut you off from their friendship. You appreciated what I said.

I don't want our love to be dragged in the mud.

───────────

I don't want to make love with you anymore. If it's over, if you don't want to give me hope, then forget it. I am too angry. It makes me too vulnerable. You're right: it gives me hope because we are so good together, I can't believe you can do without it.

*E*very American woman I talk to tells me to throw you out. European women, wherever they are from (France, England, Italy, Spain, Russia, Romania, Hungary and so on) are also unanimous: let him live his thing, be patient, wait it out. Are you worth it? Objectively, no (unfaithful bastard, cheater, liar, cold, punitive, withholding and so on, why would I want to keep you?). At a deeper level, the level where we connect, bond, fuck, feel each other out, the level where all conventions are thrown to the wind, I don't give a damn. If you need her, go ahead, but don't deprive us of what we've got. I say fuck the shrimps, fuck conventions, fuck my self-respect, fuck my pride.

Why is it that by not treating me with respect you strip me of my own self-respect? How long will I trample my pride in the name of our love?

That's what it's about, isn't it? I am walking that edge where the drama of all relationships takes place: how much will I compromise for the sake of love? How far am I willing to go?

From now on I will refer to her in my mind as the Second Wife, or the Concubine.

It is the oldest story in the world.

If we were Chinese you would keep us both. You would visit us on alternate days. If you were Arab we would live together in the harem, in separate chambers. You are, after all, Middle Eastern. Are Jews so different from Arabs? The same sensuality runs through their veins. A man with a harem. You've already got three women at home. It's an idea to entertain.

By not asking you to leave the day I found out about your affair, I took a road I had never explored before. Been there, done that, I said when you first talked about leaving, back in August. We've both broken up before. You with your ex-wife. Me with my ex-boyfriend. We both know about the pain, the agony, the grief, the patterns that get later replayed with a new lover. But we were both free when we met each other. Not breaking up now presents a new challenge. At the very least, we will find out something about ourselves, open new pathways through our emotions.

I take back what I said before. Of course I will make love with you again. How can we stop being lovers? You know the power of that bond, that's why you're so scared of it. Is that why I am accepting the situation? Because I cannot live without making love with you? Is it so primal, so powerful, that it overrides everything else? Is sex more powerful than love?

I should be your mistress.

Neither of us act according to our words. You'll have to leave, I tell you. But I haven't asked you to leave. I'm leaving, you tell me, I'm out the door. But you haven't left.

This morning, having slept nine hours of deep sleep, relaxed because—whatever that means—"I am letting you go," or "I am letting go," I am afraid that, at some unconscious level, I may have provoked this to happen. As if I was reenacting a primal scenario of abandonment.

I've never loved without fear of being abandoned, I've never loved without being afraid to lose the love. I've never loved without—at one point or another—clutching or clinging, as if I couldn't believe that a man could stay with me freely.

I am letting you go, and it's scary because you are my love. I know it's right because I sleep so well and I can finally let myself go. I am opening my arms: I don't own you. You are free.

I finally heard you: the relationship we had is over.

There's exhilaration in the gesture of letting myself drop. There's exhilaration in the fall. Feeling the body tumbling and rolling freely, feeling the muscles stretch. Not knowing where I will land but trusting, somehow, that life will welcome me.

I don't want to talk to anyone today. Talking about you is still holding on to you. Clutching the phone receiver to my ear and calling up your ghost.

Go, I think to myself. And I feel the knot loosen up inside of me.

Go, I think to myself. And I see you relax visibly in the house.

———

We cook: you make a big pot of tomato sauce with meat and I make chicken broth because you have a fever. Juliet talks to her friends on the cordless phone and watches TV nonstop. She is more angry at me than at you. From the bathroom where she is blow-drying her hair she lashes at me.

You can't even hold on to him, she yells, enraged at your rejection.

She is, like you, given to harsh declarations and provocative statements fueled by anger. She can say one thing and its opposite within a few hours, depending on her mood. I hate you, she'll say, I want to leave this house.

I am concerned about her. She's letting her schoolwork slip. I don't care anymore, she says. But she doesn't always say what she means. Or mean what she says.

Lola also, at times, decides she's had it with us and wants to move in with another family.

———

There's a routine to our days: Saturday you go out with her, and you spend part of Sunday with her. Monday you are here, cooking for the girls while I teach my class at the New School. Tuesday night is a toss-up: maybe there's some dinner or literary event she takes you to or I am going out. Maybe Wednesday you're home. Thursday or Friday you go out and meet her later.

It's reassuring when you're in the house, cooking, sleeping in our bed. But you've said it to me, over and over, in so many ways:

I am going to leave.

It's only a question of time.

Am I like a convict on death row awaiting the execution day?

And you, are you preparing your exit, taking your time, getting used to the idea, mulling it over, taking stock of our domesticity, of your children?

———

Today I am desolate, my grief hangs over the city in gray streaks, the words FATAL PROGNOSIS carved in the air.

———

Our relationship, as we know it, is over. I'm out the door. I'm leaving.

Your words sink into my gut like a death toll.

Someone said the loss of a lover is a reminder of our mortality.

Why are you running away from me so?

Is it because of an irresistible passion?

What's irresistible is what's driving you.

You've been on the run, baby, for a couple of years. Run, run, faster, faster. Out of the house, on your bike, away, away. Away from your demons that you believe are lurking in your office, everywhere in this house.

A man on the run.

There hasn't been one place in our bodies that either of us has refused to explore. You've been so open to me. There hasn't been one gesture or suggestion, erotically, that either of us has shied away from.

Why is it that we cannot do the same with our feelings? You are surrounded with barbed wire and DO NOT TRESPASS signs. An incendiary look from you, your face shutting down, your back turned to me, a threatening *Catherine!* or you walking away in the middle of a conversation signal that I have ventured on forbidden territory. Sexually, there is no forbidden territory. Emotionally: you're a closed fist.

So I lose my spontaneity around you, there are too many mines to avoid. It is forbidden to talk about fear and vulnerability, it is forbidden to cry, to show my needs, to demand anything, to worry about anything at all. It is forbidden to talk about ambivalence, to question motivations, to delve into the recesses of our souls.

We make love again. It's the place we take refuge in because we don't know anymore how to speak to each other.

A phone call comes from my agent telling me I am getting a ten-thousand-dollar check from Germany for a paperback sale. I burst into tears on the phone. I sob into the receiver. Thank God. Thank God. It's been so long since I've made any money from my writing. I run into your arms and cry on your shoulder—to hell with the fear of crying, of being like your mother. I have so much pain, I say, sobbing into your neck. What I'm going through is so hard.

You hold me with only one arm, the other one hanging by your side. You don't want to commit to a full embrace. Half of your body is warm and tender and the other half rigid and terrified.

A bomb exploded in the Paris subway yesterday, métro Palais Royal. Last week a couple of teenage sweethearts threw their newborn baby into a trash can and are now indicted for murder. The news comes to me muffled and distant, my pain buffeting me from outside reality.

We are camping in the wreckage of our love, stepping around the pieces blown apart by the bomb, going on with our daily life without the frame of a fixed relationship, creating new ground rules as we go along.

───────

I am involved with another person and it's very, very serious.

I cannot imagine saying these words to you, but you said them in front of my shrimp. You brandish them whenever you think I am pushing for a reconciliation, or whenever you feel the pull toward me.

So go! What are you waiting for? If it's such a beautiful love affair, what the fuck are you doing here? And if, for whatever reason, you have to stay here, why do you need to torture me with these words?

If I were in love with someone else, I would downplay it to spare your pain. If I were in love with someone else, I would have left already.

I don't believe that you're staying out of love for me. Maybe out of duty for the kids. You adore them. I can see the love in your eyes, in your smile, I can hear the tenderness in your voice.

Maybe you're afraid of the ultimate transgression: you, the self-proclaimed family man, are about to walk away from the family you created.

Maybe you're hoping that I will boot you out if you repeat your love for her often enough. If you refuse to give me an inch, an ounce of hope.

*Y*our face was a mask of pain at the shrimp's, the pain screaming through the anger. You tried so hard, you said, your rage barely contained, you were such a good father. But you were not a good mother for Juliet, you said to me. I was there for her. I was there for you.

Do you mean that I wasn't there for you? I always thought I was taking care of you while you took care of Juliet. You were my child, and she was yours. I thought I was a better lover than a mother, that I knew how to take care of a man better than a child. Did I let you down when I took care of Juliet more, after I started the therapy? Is that when things began to shift between us: when I became a more involved mother? Is that when I started failing you?

All these nurturing issues are too knotted. I don't know who was supposed to be the mother, the father, the children, and to whom. Were we both of us competitive about everything, about our work, about Juliet, about Lola, even?

On the FDR Drive, coming back from uptown, you say: I want to hold you in my arms.

*Y*ou went out for a walk. I am sobbing at my desk. I cannot bear to know that you love someone else. I cannot take it. I cannot live through it. I want to explode everything, leave the apartment, never come back, never see you again in my life.

———

*J*uliet dyed her hair black by mistake. The Clairol box said dark brown. The hair came out jet-black.

Like Cleopatra, I look like fucking Cleopatra!

She is screaming and sobbing, slamming doors behind her in rage and frustration. The smell in the bathroom where she and her friend were applying the dye with clear plastic gloves reminds me of the blend of hydrogen peroxide and ammonia that wafted from the bathroom when my mother was doing her monthly dye job. I dyed my hair jet-black too, when I was the same age as Juliet, fifteen or sixteen, and cut thick black bangs over my fore- head, but at the time I was hoping to look like Liz Taylor.

It's girl heaven here, or hell, depending on one's point of view.

We were man and wife. For me it was forever. Our love. The thing, whatever it was we had, the passion. A passion like that can never die.

People say: one year to recover from a love affair. Or maybe two years.

But you will never suffer from heartbreak from me. You're in love with someone else. You will never feel the pain, the loss of my love.

You will slip our relationship—almost nineteen years—under the rug.

A sleight of hand.

Well, congratulations. You have masterminded a nice little trick here. You've painlessly slipped from one woman to the other.

Despair. Ready to buy plane tickets for the girls and me to anywhere. Paris probably. And never come back. Never see you again. *I am involved with someone and it's very, very serious.* The words obliterating everything else you said. Your anger poured over me. The image you have of me: fragile, underachiever, a loner with- out friends, socially inhibited. Yes, I can be like that when I am depressed, when I am miserable. But not when I am happy. What distorted mirror, what witch's mirror are you holding up to me? I never want to see you again. I'll sell the apartment. Or burn it to the ground. Start a new life. Far, far away.

Walk into the sunset with your new paramour. Be a major success. Move into a huge loft with her. Make millions of dollars with her at your side. Start a new family. Go. Go ahead. What the fuck are you waiting for?

You'll never see us again.

If I stay I will throw all your furniture out the window and maybe mine too and start from scratch. Paint everything white. Fumigate. Exorcise.

After a couple of tequila sunrises with my Cuban friends I start to mellow out. There's a woman there who's going through a divorce and she looks good, an ex-model, half-Jamaican, and she has moved into a new apartment with her six-year-old little girl. She seems okay. Not devastated, but cool, in control. Yeah, I can do it. She says you've got to have a good lawyer and recommends hers, $275 a pop (an hour? a minute? who knows?). The best, she says. She got her husband to pay for the kid's school tuition and all of her rent.

When I came back last night you held me in your arms all night long. We didn't say a word. You made love to me with your hands and we fell asleep in each other's arms. We'd wake up once in a while and change position and hold on to each other. In the early morning you pressed yourself inside of me and came. I could feel your cum stick between my thighs when I woke up later, still nested in your arms.

———

$\mathcal{I}$ oscillate between being crazy in love with you and dripping with disdain for you. It must be what one calls a love-hate relationship. I didn't know about the hate part, until now.

$\mathcal{W}$hen I act angry at you like you do at me you can't stand it and you start spilling your venom all over me. Your voice is sour with sarcasm. About nothing. About book publishing, about film actors, about writing. It's as if you retained the ultimate knowledge about American pop culture and I was some kind of Eurotrash bumpkin who didn't have a clue. Watching *To Die For*, Gus Van Sant's movie, last night, you asked me, pointing to Matt Dillon: do you know who he is? I said yes, of course. Pointing to Nicole Kidman: do you know who she is? I lost a point there. I didn't recognize her. Nicole Kidman, you said. Oh, sorry, touché. I didn't know. She's Tom Cruise's wife, you said. Yes, I know. I knew that. And this actress, you point to the one with the straight black hair and the strong nose, do you know who she is? No. It's Illeana Douglas, Martin Scorsese's girlfriend.

Every day is an American pop culture test. They are getting harder and harder and I am failing half of them.

It's the same with writers. You've got all the inside dope on the publishing business, of course, the big and the small deals. There's nothing that you don't know. Nothing that I can surprise you with. If I come up with some inside information of my own, you make a point of correcting me. I don't really have it right. Or if I do, you act surprised: where did you get that from, who told you? If I defend the underdog, the literary writer, the downtown writer, the underground writer, or whatever that species is, you make a speech telling me with a threatening edge to your voice that the underground doesn't exist anymore. That literary writers better adapt. And quick. That publishers are not in the business of publishing literature for its own sake, but only of making money. And it's not the editors' fault.

I feel the power gather inside of me. A force pulsing.

One day I will decide it's over and you'll be in for a surprise. You won't expect it because I know how to keep my cards close to my vest. My anger barely skims the surface. In fact, I like to keep it in check because I don't want to let it leak, inadvertently triggering useless fights. Anger, in my opinion, is only good for one thing: for use as fuel to propel you forward. So I will let it pile up until it spontaneously ignites. Out, out through the stratosphere. I may not be a good fighter, but I know how to break up.

You don't know that about me, do you, that I can turn on a dime from love to good-bye, and that it will be over, really over in a second.

You don't know that about me.

That when I have reached the end of my patience, of my love—which takes me a long time—I take off like a rocket and I don't turn back.

You may think that's what you are doing, but you're not. Your ammunitions are wet, baby. You squander your strengths by getting angry, fantasizing, talking, mulling things over, trying to convince yourself out-loud. You know what we always say about writing: if we talk too much about it, we lose it, we can't write the book anymore?

I only talk about one thing: the possibility of reconciliation. My love for you. And it's still here. Sometimes. A lot of the times. But there's another side to me. A side you know nothing about. A side I show to nobody. A side of me that's implacable once it's been set in motion. So I am careful. I don't drudge up the heavy artillery unless I have used all my other weapons. Until I am absolutely sure. And then there's no hesitation. No dillydallying. No wishy-washying. No stumbling. It's very delicate, really. Thoughtful. There's no slamming of doors, no grandstanding, no seething, no outpouring. I will, very gently, pull my needle out of the game—to use the French phrase. In this case, our game.

I won't even tell you. One day you will see me alone, or with another man, walking happily down the street, my hair blowing in the wind, or sitting at the terrace of a café (yes, there are terraces in New York), and you will notice that I am glowing and carefree. You will realize—with a shock or maybe not—that I have gotten over you.

I don't know when that will be. Maybe you'll have to leave for that to happen. Because there's still all that passion between us, hot, scary, powerful; enough, it seems, to last us a lifetime.

Except we are watching each other now. Careful not to go too far. Not to make an irretrievable move. You respecting my schedule, taking your responsibilities around the house, with the kids. Me, holding my anger back. After your anger pours out you come into my arms. We are preserving something between us. We are not breaking up. You have your exit door and now I have mine: freedom. If I want to.

I wonder which one of us holds the key to what is left of our love. I'll take a chance to say: neither one. I don't think one of us has the power to kill it without the other.

This relationship refuses to die.

ᵧou took Juliet to McDonald's and asked her how she would feel if you were leaving. I don't know, she said. When she told me about your conversation she looked sullen, angry. You guys should talk to each other, she said, not to me.

You are hammering another nail in the coffin of our love.

$\mathcal{I}$f you leave, I will take your head and smash it against our front door until your brain explodes and gray matter sticks all over the walls and ceiling. I want to hear the cracking of the bones, see the back of your skull splitting open and your face disfigured, pissing blood, teeth flying, your hair matted with the innards of your cortex, maybe you could make dreads easily with that sticky gooey matter.

Her, the concubine, I would take with a gun, a .38 aimed straight at her cunt, point-blank between the lips, one end of the barrel resting against the clit and emerging out of the pube like it was growing out of dark grass. She'd be lying on her back, her legs open, ready to take you in but it would be the cold barrel of the .38. Surprise, surprise, it would be me fucking her, in and out, in and out, getting her wet, baby, she likes that, doesn't she, doesn't she like a hard cold cock, is your cock as hard as the barrel of a .38? No way. I wouldn't use a snub-nose but a long barrel, as long as your cock, in and out, in and out, cocky, you know, very cocky, fucking macho, assertive, more macho than you could ever be, what man can compete with a fucking .38, until she starts moaning, her head lolling, her lips parted, you coming, baby, you coming, here you go, pull the trigger, BANG BANG BANG, straight up her cunt, up her cervix, up her uterus, up her fucking guts, little slut, and the walls of her stomach explode and all the guts pop out, the ovaries, spilling all over her glamorous clothes, Comme des Garçons or whatever Japanese designer du jour she's wearing, her stupid cunt reduced to red, runny porridge, gurgling female syrup.

I'll give you pleasure, bitch, I'm just as good at it as he is.

———

*W*hat are you doing talking to your daughter like that? Asking her permission to leave? Or wanting her to tell you to stay?

What did you think she was going to do?

Give you her blessing?

Whatever makes you happy, Dad!

You deserve to be happy, Dad. You put in your time with us, blood, sweat and guts, it's only fair that you move on now. Your fate is calling you. We'll always love you, no matter what you do.

Yeah, right.

Who the fuck are you kidding?

Or maybe you thought she would burst into tears and beg you to stay. Daddy, Daddy, don't leave us. We need you. We can't live without you. Sobbing on your shoulder.

I don't know, she told you. And turned away.

To me, she said: I don't care, I don't give a fuck. Talk to each other, not to me. Leave me out of it. And gave me that hard black look, those fucking bullets she shoots me when she's mad and she's sick of our pathetic rigmarole.

She's got no respect for us, you know that?

And she's right, too.

Baby boomers we are. Children of the sixties and the seventies. Great role models we are. No fucking spine. Teenagers growing gray hair. Still looking for our identity, drifting where the wind pushes us.

*S*o I finally called the lawyer.

I have to protect myself, everybody tells me. But if you leave, I want to destroy you, not protect myself legally and financially. That seems too mild, too civilized. Lukewarm revenge. Nothing like the Biblical bloodshed which alone would give me satisfaction: shooting you and her, and then myself, in the head. Crime of passion. Our three bodies slack in front of her house, leaking blood and guts. Eyes revulsed, all the white showing, tongues hanging out of mouths. Is betrayal an act of violence?

You have tried to erase me, negate me. What would be the best way to torture you in retaliation? Mental, or physical torture?

I thought you had soul, I thought you had heart.

Are you just a traitor and a coward?

But maybe you still have a soul, still have a heart.

It's just that you don't love me anymore.

It's life.

So what are you doing here? What have you done here the last three and a half months? Why are you talking to the shrimp?

Biding your time? Waiting for money? Using your office, enjoying the presence of your children everyday, making love with me, living the family life until it's convenient for you to move out, until you've prepared your next move?

I am afraid to ask these questions. I am afraid to ask you point-blank: What are your plans? What are your intentions?

We continue to live in ambiguity, in vagueness, a world where intentions and dreams do not meet actions. And I am complicit. Even in the best of times, if there was a problem between us we would fight, you would get pissed off, wouldn't talk for two hours or three days, and then we'd make love and forget it. Anything too hot I would drop tacitly, kick it out of sight, hoping it would stay quiet. Every confrontation always hit the same wall: you walking away and sulking for hours if not days. It wasn't worth the trouble. Deep down, we trusted each other, I think. There was an unspoken agreement that we were in it for the long haul, together, no matter what the conflicts.

But now things are different. Something has happened that no amount of lovemaking can undo.

How can I believe a word of what you say? How can I trust

you in any way? Are you as treacherous toward her as you are toward me?

I could forgive you for your betrayal, but you're not asking for my forgiveness.

*T*his is turning into the passion of Jesus Fucking Christ. With you as Judas, of course. I am carrying the cross and the crown of thorns is bleeding into my hair and all over my face. And the day you leave is the day of crucifixion. Is that supposed to be my fate? Then you will have succeeded in your ritual killing.

I don't want to march to my death, patiently waiting for you to leave me.

*Y*ou are cooking again tonight, defrosting a chicken in cream sauce that you cooked a few weeks ago, preparing an early dinner because you are "going out." This is the new code word. We both know what it means. You talk about it coyly. I don't know how many more times I can take it, seeing you "go out" to fuck another woman.

4

I will give you the coup de grâce.

I will not let you leave me or abandon me. I will not wait until you are ready to move on, as you say—whether it takes weeks or months until you have enough money or your guilt has abated or whatever it is that you are waiting for—and listen to you tell me: I am leaving, I am going to live with her. I will not let you say that to me. I will not hear those words. I will move faster than you, take you by surprise and tell you to leave: by the end of the day, or the week, or the month. And remove all your belongings. Put everything in storage. All your books, your paintings, all your knickknacks, your parents' furniture, your dozens of hats hanging from the pegs in the hallway—the taupe fedora and the Persian lamb hat with the flaps, and the leather baseball cap and your father's straw Panama hat, the one you brought him back from Ecuador twenty years ago and that's all beat up now and that has become your fetish, your gris-gris, one of your many gris-gris—, your Ecuadorian blowgun and Indian arrows, the Native American headdress that your brother gave you one Christmas, all your Indian stuff, your toiletries from Kiehl's, your CDs, your boxes and boxes of paper, your comics, your manuscripts and screenplays, your Armani jackets and old sports gear, your bench press and your weights, your huge desk from the UN that you've had for thirty years, your computers, your briefcases, your old shoes and suits from the seventies, your old scarves and mittens and baseball jackets from twenty-five years ago.

Your books.

That, in itself, is quite a job. Your books and my books are so intermingled on the shelves.

I'd rather move a little too fast than risk being left.

I have taken so much pain, so much punishment. I don't know that I can take much more. I am ready—soon, very soon—to cut my losses.

The excitement of the breakup, the exquisite frisson of freedom, the headiness of moving into the unknown and starting from scratch.

———

*I*t's 11:30 P.M. Juliet sees you hover by the door, picking up your keys silently, and she comes to tell me in bed.

Where's Dad going?

By the time I come downstairs, in my bathrobe, ostensibly to pour myself a glass of water, you're sitting on the couch looking sheepish, with your boots on.

I can't stand seeing you ashamed to be caught sneaking out.

You get up and sit by the dining room table, inching toward the front door. I watch you from the bottom of the stairs for a long time. I don't know what to say. I am paralyzed. But I also want to torture you. Just by staying there, watching you, I am holding you back.

What's up, you say, without lifting your head.

I know what you're doing.

You shoot up from your seat. Put your leather jacket on.

I am leaving. That's it, I'm leaving.

Another encoded message.

I've done everything I could, you say. But it's always been about you, you, you. You never acknowledged me.

You put your hat on—the newsboy's cap.

I'm leaving, you say again.

What makes you think I want you to stay? I shoot back.

I don't. I don't know what you want.

You walk down the hallway, toward the front door.

Good-bye, you say.

Good-bye.

The door slams behind you.

I knew you wouldn't come back the whole night.

I didn't sleep at all. At seven, when I got up and went downstairs to an empty kitchen, I cried. I missed you so much. You were nowhere you should have been. Not picking up the newspaper downstairs. Not holding your mug of coffee while doing the *New York Times* crossword puzzle, not getting dressed in the bedroom. Not taking a leak in the bathroom.

At 8:30 A.M., just as I was getting Lola ready, you walked in the door.

What are you doing here?

I came to do my job, you said, take Lola to school.

When you came back I took you in my arms and sobbed.

I did everything I could too, I said. I loved you the best I knew how.

You held me tight.

When you used to hold me in your arms like this, all my fears would fall away, all my pain would go. I could always count on you, it was us against the world, you were always on my side. You defended our little clan with passion—the two of us, then the three of us, later the four of us.

It is that bond, that unshakable belief in your loyalty, that makes me still fight for you.

*I*n the afternoon—we were again sitting together at the yellow kitchen table—I said: I don't see you pack up your bags.

I was teasing you. Or maybe the right word would be: testing. I was testing you.

You didn't lift your nose from the crossword puzzle. You didn't say anything.

That night Lola came to sleep between us and at dawn you came around on my side and held me in your arms. I told you how much I missed our friendship. You said you felt how deep our bond is, sometimes.

*Y*ou're still here. It was almost a week ago.

I think you'll be here through the holidays.

I didn't give you the coup de grâce. I can't. I still love you.

———

You were lingering in the living room, tentatively, after putting Lola to sleep. I was reading a magazine on the couch. Usually when you linger tentatively it's a sign that you want to go out but dare not do it in front of me. I checked your feet: you didn't have your boots on. You sat on a chair. No, you were not leaving, you wanted to talk to me.

What you wanted to say was this: you had decided to leave after the holidays. You used the word "resolve." You said you had to follow your heart. You also said you had doubts, and that some days you couldn't imagine that you would really leave this house.

The Christmas Eve dinner was planned. Fourteen people, good friends, around the long pink table. You had already done part of the shopping, I still had some errands to do: pick up the meat at Balducci's, the cake at that French pastry up on Madison Avenue, the last Christmas presents. I knew you had spent the afternoon at her place. I thought maybe you had talked with her about finally making your move.

I was calm, relaxed.

I said: do what you have to do. If you have to leave, leave. I still love you. I don't know how long I will keep that love, but our bond is so strong, it can't go away like that.

Our bond is very strong, you said. It will never go away.

In the bedroom, I teased you: what's this new thing about keeping your underwear on?

The last two or three nights you had kept your boxers on at night, ostensibly making a statement that you were not available sexually.

Since you're going to leave anyway, I said, we might as well enjoy the last few days.

You laughed and stripped down. We held each other for a long time and made love.

Christmas Eve was dark, the pain holding my chest in a suffocating grip.

Errands had to be run, the house prepared, the table set with the antique linen from France and the silver from my grandmother and pink candles in the candlesticks, the girls dressed, my mother kept under control, the food started, and finally getting dressed and made-up myself.

The first glasses of champagne poured, the mood loosened up. It was our Christmas Eve dinner, only better. It was as if our friends were pouring heavy doses of warmth and love, keeping us together in a tightly knit web of good wishes and good humor.

During dinner you were sitting at the other end of the table, talking to a friend, but I overheard you. I heard your exact words. The same words you had used the day before. You said: I have to follow my heart.

It pissed me off that you had to talk about that at our dinner table, a few feet away from me. And I hated that expression "follow your heart." It sounded corny to me. Another cliché. I wouldn't have liked you to use it about me. I started a conversation at my end of the table. I didn't want to be witness to the anguish of your new love. An hour later, you had changed places and we all talked together and it felt like us, the energy between us and the laughs and the warmth.

The last guests left around 2 A.M. and we cleaned up together like we've always done, we've got it down pat, we work well together. After that we sat on the couch looking at the Christmas tree and you got up and gave me an envelope, and joked that this time my Christmas present was small and skinny.

It was a gift certificate for a spa on Fifth Avenue, the kind of place some of your women friends go to, maybe your girlfriend. Not the kind of place I go to myself. Usually you give me clothes or lingerie. Still, the gift certificate was a present for my body and I liked it, even though it was a little impersonal, it wouldn't be your hands touching me, but those of strangers.

I gave you your present, the pair of motorcycle boots you wanted. You put them on, walked around the Christmas tree, asked me if they looked good on you.

Did I give you boots to walk away from me?

On Christmas morning you videotaped the girls opening their presents and it was like a good Christmas again. I cooked eggs Benedict and you hovered around me, out of hunger, or maybe to check if I wasn't going to fuck up something. You don't have much faith in my cooking. I didn't fuck up. The eggs were thirty seconds overdone but fine. We sat down for brunch with my mother and the girls. After brunch we cleaned up and then you announced abruptly that you were going out and wouldn't come back for dinner. That's when I realized that you had split your Christmas in two: Christmas Eve with me and Christmas Day dinner with her.

_____

*T*his morning at the shrimp I said: we've been together a long time, it will be nineteen years this first of January. This was bound to happen. We are not meant to be monogamous for a lifetime. You have to live this love affair all the way, you've got to go to the bottom of it, see where it takes you, what it means for you.

You said she was the passport to a world you wanted very

much, a world of parties and glitter that you weren't sure you could get without her, that you weren't sure you could have access to just on the strength of your talent. You added that you liked her a lot too, that you were not using her.

It makes sense, I said. She's the right woman to accompany you on that trip, with that book.

You said you were afraid of my anger.

I told you I had changed in the last couple of weeks, that I didn't feel that anger right now.

You said that after you leave you want to take care of the kids, take Lola to school in the morning, shop for us, be part of their caretaking and the household.

I said you could keep the keys to the house and you could come and see the girls but you'd have to call first.

After the session we went to a little French café on Thompson Street, the one whose owners are friends with the owners of the olive oil mill in my mother's village in Provence. We ordered croque-monsieurs and cappuccinos and I said, if I was American, I would probably not act this way, we are doing this the French way, and we laughed.

You said you would leave after the holidays. I take it you mean right after the first, which is a Wednesday, and since you plan to be with her for New Year's Eve I ask you if you would spend the last four days of the year with us and you say yes. We make a date for dinner for the two of us on Monday night.

———

On Saturday night I find you baking a big meat loaf studded with green pepper and herbs and you tell me you have invited our Cuban friends and their little girls, who are friends of Lola's. We drink wine and beer and it's like old times again, we're home together, having fun around the long pink Formica table, and on Sunday you spend most of the day at home and the four of us feel whole again.

Things are better between you, right? Juliet asks. And she decides to clean up her room. She takes out armloads of paper and old notebooks dating back ten years and calls me at the end of the day to show me this unbelievable miracle: drawers emptied out, shelves rearranged, floor entirely free of clothes, shoes, makeup, chewing-gum wrappers, dirty socks, heaps of wet bath towels, hair brushes, hair-dryer, CDs: a clear path from door to bed, the rug entirely visible, sweaters neatly folded and piled on the shelves, blouses and skirts hanging, color-coordinated, on their hangers.

Peace. Saying good-bye in peace. Except the girls don't know it will be good-bye. Are you going to send them to the gas chamber pretending they're just going to take a shower?

⎯⎯⎯⎯

$\mathcal{T}$oday is mild, unbelievably mild for the end of the year, and sunny, balmy almost, like an early spring day.

Warm enough for a bike ride? you ask me, always ready to speed out into the ozone to forget everything.

You take the BMW out, and I believe it's true, this time, that you're going for a bike ride, that it's not another code word for taking the bike out to her place.

In the evening, while I wait for you—tonight is our good-bye dinner—I feed the girls and my mother, who's back from her friends' place on the Upper East Side and will stay until New

Year's Eve. The usual, pasta and the tomato sauce that you cooked yourself. I sit down for a glass of red Burgundy with my mother, and I have a little cheese with her.

Now it's past eight o'clock—not that it matters, we always have late dinners, and I haven't made a reservation anywhere—but I wonder if you're going to show up. For a few minutes I have the feeling you might not want to face me for this dinner, that you'd rather slip out into the night, into another life. Like one of these guys who—one finds out years later, sometimes thirty years later—have another woman and another family in another city, or in another part of town, or do not come back home one day and set up house with their new lover.

But at eight-thirty you walk in the door and your face looks more serene, the furrows between your eyes smoothed, you have a general air of benevolence and warmth. We get dressed and take the car and go to a fish restaurant on Avenue A and right away everything feels right. We share a plate of mussels with a spiked sauce, and you are the first one to talk: so what's up with us, Catherine? You say Catherine with the stress on the second syllable, the French way, the way you say it when you are feeling warm and loving toward me.

And it feels like us again, we joke and once again you say you have no idea what you're doing and what's going to happen. And once again I say things that I've said before, words to alleviate your crushing guilt and my own pain, and at that moment, your guilt seems to have lifted and I don't feel any pain but a lot of love and warmth and I can't believe that I still love you through all this, I don't know if love is the right word, maybe it's just that there is this dance we know how to do, when our energies hook up and things click between us and the chemistry is right there—not just sexual, but sparks of electricity zapping around us.

After dinner we get up to have a cigarette at the bar, and we perch on two stools and smoke your Marlboro Lights. This affair is a major bonus for the tobacco industry. You took up smoking a little before you started going out with her, or maybe just about that time, and I—who had not smoked for sixteen years, who had stopped when I was pregnant with Juliet in Montreal, wrecked with all-day sickness—have started to smoke again, when I go out.

We sit very close to each other, like lovers do, but of course we are lovers. And this is what you say to me: to tell you the truth, I have no idea where this is going with her, it could be wonderful or it could be a nightmare. And I think of that line from an Eagles song: "This could be heaven or this could be hell." And then you betray her a little bit and you say: her tack is to put no pressure on me. I laugh and say: yeah, it's the right tack in her position. And you say: she thinks you're smart the way you're doing it. And I laugh again: rivals appreciating each other. You realize we are rivals, right? She trying to get you, me trying to keep you? We laugh together about that.

And then you say: bear with me for three, four months and I'll see what happens.

I pull a long drag on the Marlboro and I have to ask you three times because I almost choke as I exhale: do you mean to say that you might want to come back? And you say: I might. And I ask you: So it would be like a tryout? And you say yes. You've never said that before, and somehow, because of the closeness between us and the little sparks of electricity, I take it to mean that at that moment you are thinking that yes, you might want to come back if things don't work out.

I'd like to leave all my stuff and furniture here and just pack a bag and take my computer with me, you say.

I have my hand on your neck and I rub it against the back of your skull that's buzzed tight. I feel the prickles of hair with my fingers as you lean into my palm, smiling your smile and kissing me, lightly, on the lips.

And as I kiss you, I think I know what you're doing: you're conning me. You're like this Moroccan guy I met at the post office in Marrakech, who seduced me with his promise to take me to a Berber wedding and who ended up trying to rape me in a hotel room at 5 A.M. There's a part of me that falls for these promises. That's a weakness I have: if you tell me what I want to hear, I'll fall for it. If you tell me with enough heart, I'll believe it. You're good at that, at pouring the right amount of emotion at the right time. It's your charm, your seduction. You can move anybody to tears. You can win their hearts. You are the consummate actor. You are wonderful at spinning stories and make-believe worlds. Maybe that's what you meant that time when you told me that you don't always mean what you say.

And you know I want to believe you. I so want to believe you. Maybe, at this instant, you even believe yourself.

I don't know if you calculate any of this. I think that you've got an infallible instinct, that you know you've got me here. You know I'm still desperate for you. I've given you all the cards and you are playing them one by one.

I take another long drag of the cigarette. I let you play me because I want to hear what you said, I still cling to that wisp of hope. So I don't say anything. I just tease you, accuse you of having gotten me to smoke again, it's all your fault.

At this moment everything seems simple to me. You're going on a trip, you pack your bag and your computer and live out your affair, and I see it fall apart within a few months. I float on this unexpected hope, a small pink cloud drifting through the storm: things fall apart between you and her, and you want to come back.

We make love when we go home, my whole body stretched out on top of you, my arms along yours, my hands pressing hard into your open palms, pinning them against the pillow on either side of your head, the way you like it, if we had a bed post I would tie up your wrists behind your head with a silk scarf and you would groan.

Would you take him back after that?

You may not want to take him back after that.

"Take him back." As if you were a stray dog or a prodigal son. Would we want to be together again? I don't know if I would want to live with you again, subjected to the barrage of TV, your sulkiness, your flashes of rage, your sullen presence, your irritability whenever the kids fight or things don't run smoothly, your unavailability, your slipperiness.

But to be your lover? Yes, of course. You'd stop by for dinner in the evening, and after the kids are in bed we'd talk about writing, and we'd make love and you'd stay for breakfast and take the kids to school, or I would meet you at a party or at a restaurant and I'd be dressed up and you'd be in a good mood and flirtatious and we would laugh together, then I'd come back home and be on my own with the girls for a couple of days and I would be free, without you criticizing me or breathing down my neck making me feel I am doing something wrong.

Yeah, I think about that for a little while, but not too long because that's one fantasy I can't indulge in, not right now, not anymore maybe. But the feeling lingers for the whole day until it's time for you to open the oysters on New Year's Eve.

My French friends call to say they are not coming to share the oysters with us, some last-minute change of plan.

You tense up when I tell you this, because that means we're going to be alone with my mother, but you don't say anything. The girls pick up the tension and zap it back and forth aimlessly. It comes back at us like a boomerang. I get dressed, but when I come down I find you sitting at the dinner table in a sweatshirt, hunched over the crossword puzzle, your shoulders rounded and sideways, spelling: DON'T COME NEAR ME. STAY AWAY.

Subtlety is the only way if I want to avoid a fight. I pull the bags of oysters from the fridge and put them on the counter next to the oyster pick, this short contraption shaped like a tiny scimitar that you've learned to use deftly, holding the oyster in the left hand wrapped in a dishcloth.

I am taking the oysters out, I tell you. They are right there on the counter.

I walk out of the kitchen, hoping you'll get the message. But you make a point of ignoring me and I know your silence means trouble.

You finally open the oysters and we eat them with champagne, but the mood is heavy. My mother is trying to engage you in conversation, but I can see the signs of rage and impatience surfacing in the way your face tightens and your foot starts tapping nervously. I am wearing a tight and fluid black silk dress and high heels, and I drink champagne as if this were like all the New Year's Eves that we've spent together.

Tomorrow, January 1, it will be nineteen years since we met.

It was a New Year's Day dinner party on the Upper West Side. You had showed up after dinner and sat on the floor next to me. Even though you had just had your hair cut, you still had a big head of tight curls, seventies-style. We started talking, and right away it was as if our bodies were irresistibly pulled to each other by a powerful magnet. Later, we all walked out together in the snow, and by the time we had gotten to the Seventy-second

Street station, or was it the Sixty-sixth Street station, there was a soft carpet of pristine white all over the ground and we kissed, cold lips and hot breaths. Our shoulders were covered with snowflakes, I was wearing a forties mouton fur coat that I had bought secondhand in Montreal, and the flakes gathered on the collar, dripping into my neck.

The next day I went to see *Star Wars* in a Times Square movie theater, and I called you when I got out. We met that night in a little bar on Amsterdam Avenue and your fingers traced arabesques in the palm of my hand. We were making out right there with our hands between the glasses of scotch. We walked back to your friend's apartment to make love, my hand in the back pocket of your jeans. You were wearing your green satin baseball jacket (it's still hanging in our closet) with the words PASSAIC DE MOLAY stitched in white letters on the back, and you had to explain to me what it meant.

You were the American of my dreams. A New York Jew with horn-rimmed glasses and a sensual mouth, and the sexiest smile. Tall, lanky, wild and dangerous. Funny. And so tender. My body fell into yours as if diving to the bottom of the ocean. The next morning I was flying back to Montreal and you to LA. I never thought, that day, that our love affair would take us so far, across several continents and cities, from LA to New York to Montreal to Paris to North Africa and back to New York; and that it would grow and take root and flourish like it did.

*B*ut tonight you have a date with her, and at nine-thirty you start shifting on the couch and you say you have to go, and Lola asks you, where are you going Dad, and you tell her: I'm having dinner with friends. I wonder what she is expecting you with, more champagne, caviar, smoked salmon, or a bottle of Laphroaig, your favorite scotch?

I walk you to the hallway while you put on the new motorcycle boots I have given you for Christmas, and your leather jacket.

Happy New Year, I tell you.

But the happy new year I am wishing you is a year with me, not a year with her.

Happy New Year, you whisper, and we kiss gently on the lips.

I knew you wouldn't come back that night. I don't think you had told me, or if you had I hadn't heard, sometimes one hears only what one wants, but I knew it in my bones and when I woke up at 2:30 A.M.,—my sleep is hardwired to break around 2 A.M., the way it was when the girls were infants and ready to be nursed, but now it's the time when you usually walk in on your way back from her place—and listened to the silence in the apartment, I knew you weren't there. I stayed up until 4 A.M. and wondered if this was it, if you were gone for good. I took two little Chinese sleeping pills, and then a third one, and sunk into a deep sleep.

You walked in around 1 P.M. the next day, as if nothing had happened. You should have told me you weren't coming back last night, I said, and you said I thought you knew, and I felt as if you were slipping away some more.

In our hallway are hung a series of photographs of the four of us taken by a photographer friend. Family portraits that you asked her to take at a time when you had already drilled a crack into the family. Why did you want these pictures taken? I can only speculate. Maybe for the same reasons I was setting pictures of you and me all over the apartment: as a talisman against the dissolution of our love? The photos were shot in the photographer's studio last winter, about a year ago.

On these pictures you wear your taupe fedora and one of

your Armani jackets and your shades, and you look like a movie star playing the part of a handsome and raffish writer from the forties, and Juliet and Lola and I look like refugees from Ellis Island, the family that you have just picked up at the deck. You stand apart a little, as if there was a wedge between you and us and you were not sure you, a man from the new world, a new American, wanted to be associated with us, your family from the old country. These are extraordinary pictures and they tell a story, except none of us knew at the time what story they were telling, perhaps you didn't even know yourself.

There were seven pictures originally, hanging on the wall of our narrow hallway, fragile in their glass frames held by a tiny nail, and they tend to fall and the glass frames break if someone walks by in a big winter jacket. Two have already bit the dust.

Nobody is replacing the missing pictures. I wonder how long it will take until all of them shatter to the ground.

On Friday, at the shrimp session, you deny that you've said: bear with me, give me three-four months and I might come back.

If I mentioned a time, I shouldn't have, you say, because I have no idea what's going to happen.

It made me angry that you were denying what you had said. Maybe you misunderstood him, the shrimp said. Maybe I did. But what is the point of trying to talk if words can be misinterpreted, if they can be taken back, if they blow like feathers in the wind? No wonder I only trust the language of the body. I don't agree with your shrimp. Sex doesn't lie. Bodies don't lie. Words lie. They are as treacherous as feelings.

Once, way back when we had first met, one of your woman

friends said—maybe out of jealousy—that you were unreliable and irresponsible. You didn't mind that she said that, I think. I remember that it had made you laugh. That was your reputation back then: you were a flirt, a child-man, a free spirit, a pure artist who would never take a straight job. And I didn't mind either. I wanted you to be wild, and irresponsible and free. It made you sexier.

And yet you built a house and a magazine and a family with me. Which is the real you?

———

*F*riday is the turning point for me.

I don't want you to wait for me, you say, I don't know what I'm doing.

Fine. I am not waiting for you. I am not waiting for you to come back. I am not even waiting for you to leave.

I start cleaning up the apartment top to bottom. I throw out three trash bags, I drop off four garbage bags full of old clothes at the Salvation Army thrift shop. I buy a new lamp with a lampshade encrusted in amber-colored glass and shells for the living room. I also buy a new set of sheets—cream-colored poplin, pristine—to put on the bed the day you leave. To start my new life without you. I cannot bear the idea of sleeping in the sheets in which we have made love so much. I want a virgin pair of sheets. I place the shopping bag of sheets at the back of my closet, secretly. It's only for me to know. A private symbol of freedom.

The sheets are still in the closet.

Today, Tuesday, late afternoon, you stop at the door of my office.

I want to talk to the girls tonight, you say.

My heart tears a little, but the wound is clean.

I talked about it with the shrimp this morning, you say. I want to do it while I have the courage.

So we prepare dinner together—the staples: pasta and to-mato sauce again—and I can feel you gear up for the talk. But Juliet has a big essay to write on the history of the United Na-tions and she needs my help to take notes from the CD-ROM encyclopedia and translate them into French, and you decide to wait until she's done and put Lola to bed. By the time we're finished with the history homework, you're asleep on Juliet's bed and I know the talk won't be for tonight.

 $\mathcal{O}$ n Wednesday I bring my mother back to our apartment to pack her luggage and get her into a cab for the airport, and then you go out another night for drinks with your publicist. You'll talk to the girls on Friday, you say, and leave after the weekend, but I go out on Friday, and then on Saturday we both go out—although not together—and now it's Sunday, and I'm ready for you to leave.

I am reclaiming my space, I think, pissing at every room corner like a tomcat. Getting rid of clutter. Burning incense sticks and candles to cleanse the air.

I go out to see the rewrite of Sam Shepard's early play *Tooth of Crime*, a series of riffs on being a male in America. In the dark I write down a quote on my Playbill: "all strut, no gut." I wonder what defines a man. If it's the strut or the guts. If some men might be confusing one with the other. I thought you and I could take turns being male and female like we do as lovers, but when I played the feminine role, cocooning at home, my mind focused on the kids and the house, you took off like a rocket, coming on to women and treating me with disdain, in the purest macho tradition.

The whole week I have relished my newfound freedom: you will not criticize me when I back up across a street to get into a parking spot; you will not criticize me if dinner is not ready when you are hungry; you will not criticize me if the girls are fighting or if Juliet watches TV for five hours straight, lounging on the couch; you will not snap at me for liking a movie or a book that you deem unworthy of praise; you will not ignore me with a wall of silence if I touch a nerve or unwittingly push one of your buttons.

How did we get to that place where you turned against me? I have no idea. If I tried to trace the time, I would say sometime around two years ago, when you took your editing job; you snapped, you disconnected from me, out of anger, out of frustration; you dropped out. We short-circuited. But maybe the roots go further back, to the beginning of our relationship, to your mother and your father and my mother, roots so ancient and deep and thick there was no way we could clear a path through them.

5

In the backyard, from the window, the vegetable and flower lots covered with snow look like rows of children's tombstones in a graveyard. It was summer when I came back from France, when you told me you didn't love me anymore.

Summer. Fall. Winter. Three seasons already; are we going to hold the siege until spring?

In the résumés that I prepare to apply to various writers' colonies, I delete the line saying that I live with you and our two daughters. I take out all mention of our family. I just keep the sentence: she lives in New York City.

We've been saying good-bye for more than two weeks now. Our *dîner d'adieux* was on December 30. It was ten days ago that you stepped into my office, looking grim and determined, and told me you were going to talk to the girls "tonight." You said you would leave on Friday. Friday has come and gone. The new sheets are stashed at the back of my closet, waiting for the night you will leave. When we made love during the weekend, I thought it might be for the last time, as if you were going to war. My face was pressed against your cheek and I held back the tears.

I'll miss you, I said into your neck. I'll miss you so much.

You didn't say anything.

What do you feel about me, I asked you.

I don't know.

A little while later, I asked you again:

Are you sad to leave?

I am horribly sad, you said, and you sounded desperate.

In the night, while you sleep, I steal kisses on your shoulder.

When you leave, it will be as if you had died.

I have installed a bookcase in your office. I couldn't stand looking at the piles of books teetering all over. You like the bookcase, even though you will not use it, since you're leaving. You carry armloads of paperbacks to put on the shelves.

You say: if we have an intern, we can have him alphabetize all the books.

You've said that before, not so long ago. You love your books. Your books and my books are together on all the shelves, French and American literature, intermingled and entwined. You sit on the bottom step of the stairs and you look at the open kitchen.

I love these arches, you say.

You made them yourself, out of plaster. You shaped them with your own hands like a sculpture. They are painted a dusty Mediterranean blue, like arches in an Arab town, where the dazzling whitewashed walls turn bluish in the shade.

We made this apartment our home. We call it a house, not an apartment, because of its two stories, and the brick walls, and the wooden staircase, and all the windows. It feels like a country house.

It would be beautiful to have another arch going into the kitchen, you say. You could make it the width of the bookcase.

I notice that you say "you" and not "we."

Last Sunday it was only the two of us in the morning. Both girls had sleepovers. You brought me breakfast in bed, like you used to do on weekend mornings. Coffee and scones and my favorite orange marmalade. I was surprised and happy.

But a couple of hours later I printed a paper requesting from the board of directors of our corporation that the shares of our apartment be put into my name. A month ago you said I could have the apartment if you left. I was shaky when I called you into my office and asked you to sign the request. I felt I had to do it. I was scared that I might lose the apartment.

Your face tightened and you grabbed the pen I handed you and furiously scribbled your signature. You picked up your leather jacket and your hat, and I followed you to the door.

Are you coming back for dinner?

I doubt it, you said, angrily.

I thought that this time you were leaving for good. But you came back for dinner, and again you didn't "talk" to the girls.

———

*A*t night, I dreamed about your brother. By a weird coincidence, during the day he had called to say that his wife was leaving him. In the dream he was small and frail and he was pulling his teeth out of his gums one by one with his fingers. He had a bleeding wound around his heart, as if he had been shot in the chest. In the opening of his shirt I could see he was also bleeding from his guts, from another gunshot. He was teetering, could barely stand on his feet. When I woke up I wondered if the dream was about me, but I felt strong and whole.

*A*t the shrimp session this morning you said I was cleaning out the apartment and you thought you'd be next, tossed out on the street like a garbage bag. It was sweet and funny and wry, and I loved you for saying that so bluntly.

Later you told me you had been thinking about staying, that you were terrified to start a new relationship and you couldn't bear to leave your daughters. You said I was taking charge of my life, which is what you wanted me to do, but you were concerned that if we stayed together and we had a fight in three years, you might be sorry you didn't get out when you had an opportunity.

I don't believe that you are calculating your moves that coldly. You are like an animal caught in a trap and fighting blindly, ferociously. Only when you talk about your daughters, when you look at them with tears in your eyes, do I recognize the man I love, and my heart breaks.

I will not change anything in my life. No matter what you do I will forge ahead and write, and raise our daughters and support them and have a life. With or without you.

*T*onight I went to a reading and then to see Chabrol's *La Cérémonie*. You went to see her. I wonder what you tell her, if she's getting pissed at you for being unable to make up your mind, or if she's playing the role of the loving and understanding woman.

But I only think of her for a brief instant and then I forget her, because I like to dive into the world, not as half of a couple but complete. I like to feel my body struggling alone in the cold, without you at my side to protect and stifle me simultaneously. And yet, all evening, I felt giddy and warm hoping that you might want to stay.

———

*Y*ou didn't manage to kill me. Does it mean I am the one who's going to kill you? Can we both survive this breakup?

Last night, when you told me after dinner that you were "going out," I had a moment of barely controlled fury. So you're going to settle back into your affair and stay? What makes you think you're still welcome here, after having told me that you were "leaving" two Fridays ago? I am using quote marks around these words: "going out," "staying," "leaving." The words are so heavy they bend under their own weight. They mean too much. The only act that you can really manage is "going out."

I put away a photograph of both of us—one that I had set on one of my bookshelves last year—a futile gesture, as futile as setting the picture up on the shelf in the first place. Life cannot be frozen in objects and symbols, it's a powerful movement forward. The voracious energy propelling me right now, that's life: the survival instinct, stepping over the dying body of our old relationship. Insolent, obscene, furiously selfish, cruel. The killer instinct.

*I*t's no longer a tender energy. It's wild and violent and ruthless. And sarcastic and wry and sly. The energy that makes me write, that makes me fuck. It's primal and I don't know how to tame it.

I have come out of my wifey cocoon and men are hitting on me like they used to. But men in their forties have thinning hair or a pouch and look too mature or set in their ways, too fatherly. I like men like you, or like you used to be, men with that lanky teenage look and unpredictability, ready to take off or blow a fuse. I am waiting for the spark, the sexual fire. I don't know if I'll ever find a lover as good with me as you are. As sensual as you are. I look at men and appraise them: their smiles, the color of their eyes, the way their muscles move, how much they make me laugh, if I feel the pull to stretch out next to them, if I like their hands. I'm afraid I will never be able to replace you. I cannot imagine how you could have replaced me.

I didn't know you liked redheads. Her red is "out of a bottle," she told me one day at a party. It was the second time I met her. The party was in Williamsburg, Brooklyn. It was a year and a half ago, a couple of days before I left for France, at the end of July. The reason I remember the date of that party is that you started going out with her only a few days later. There was nothing between you and her yet, but I could feel vibes. I could feel sexual vibes between you and every other woman as well, you were on the prowl and available. I camped next to you the whole evening, a pitiful attempt to chain you to me, and you obliged, which surprised me. We smoked a joint and got stoned and hung out together. Maybe the knowledge that you would be free just a few days later gave you the patience to put up with me.

I don't know why she and I talked about our hair. The animosity I felt toward her was thick and poisonous. I don't know what she felt about me. But we did what women do in that case: we exchanged syrupy banalities and checked out each other's clothes.

My red is from henna, darker than hers. My hair is thick and curly, wild around my face, hers is long and straight, parted in the middle. I wonder what else she has in common with me. The most obvious: we are both sexy and vivacious and vibrant, and we both laugh easily. For the rest, I don't have a clue. Did she grow up in the suburbs like you did? I cannot imagine a suburban American childhood. I do not know the code words, I can only imagine the complicity, the jokes, the giggles you might share at the simple utterance of a TV-series character, or a turn of phrase or some sports reference. Do you buy her sexy lingerie like you buy me? Or are your gifts "friendship" gifts, more serious, as befits a writer to his editor?

—————

𝒪n Saturday you left in the morning, saying you were going to see an early screening of a movie. At five in the afternoon, Lola, who remembers everything, asked me, where's Dad? His movie is so long. I told her the movie was probably over by now.

I think Dad is living somewhere else, she said.

𝓘 had driven by her house that afternoon. To see where you live with her. It was easy to find her address. She's in the book. She lives on a quiet block of row houses.

I have written the number on a yellow Post-it, crumpled in my pocket. I slow down, ease behind a Budget rental truck. Here it is: a four-story house, plain brick facade, green door, next to a convent. How ironical. She's a Catholic, like me. The name of the convent is carved into the white stone surrounding the door. I look up, trying to guess which floor she lives on. I don't see your motorcycle parked on the street. It's too cold. You must have left it in the garage.

It's 3:15 P.M. I imagine you and her making love behind one of these windows. Or maybe her bedroom is at the back, she must have a floor-through. I try to picture the small rooms, the period detail around the doorways, the windows, the moldings that you see when you lie on your back and she mounts you. Or maybe you never look at the moldings, but you devour her face, her skin, with your eyes.

I slowly drive down the street. There's a little French café on the corner. I look through the windows to see if you might be there with her having a late brunch. I drive around the block, looking for you on the avenue, preparing for the shock of seeing you next to her, perhaps your arm around her shoulders, or the two of you walking hand in hand. But I only see the anonymous Saturday afternoon crowd. I drive again past her door. I pull up behind the truck. I imagine you walking up the stoop at night, your heart beating, she waiting for you. You must have a key to her front door, I could take it from your key ring, come on a weekday and steal inside her apartment, check out her furniture, her beauty products, her brand of tampons, the hair color she uses for her hair, her underwear.

You didn't come back in the evening. I thought you might come to pick up the car but you didn't. We rented videotapes and got a pizza. When it was time to put Lola to bed, I lost my temper. She was cranky, too tired. It was getting late. I imagined you in her walk-up, making love to her on her couch, your hand coming up her thigh, slipping under the elastic of her panties. Lola was acting up, refusing to put her pajamas on. I pulled on her sweatshirt, a hard yank, my nails scratched her belly by accident. She fell on her butt, screaming. You hurt me, Mom, she yelled, it hurts. She pulled her sweatshirt up to reveal two thin scratches. She ran to her sister and took refuge in her arms. What did you do to her, Juliet asked accusingly. I sat next to them, my face in my hands, and I cried out of shame.

Every Saturday night when you go out to fuck her I am

possessed with killing rage. I am brittle. I snap at the drop of a pin. Every Saturday night it's you I want to destroy, your flesh I want to slash with my nails, your blood I want to see gush out. But you're not here. You have the nerve to walk out on us. You think because I don't say anything I tacitly accept your betrayal. But I don't. My rage will end up consuming what's left of my love for you.

Lola got two Band-Aids and asked me to put them on the scratches. She curled into my arms on her bed, and I read her a book and held her tight against me until she fell asleep.

Juliet refused to speak to me, to look at me even, for the rest of the evening.

In the morning when I woke up I found you lying beside me, and I stretched my body over yours and you gave yourself to my hands, you arched your back to me. We made love. Look at me, I asked you, and you looked at me and we kissed. After we'd both come, you stayed curled inside my arms for a long time, like Lola last night.

The three of you are my children. Sometimes it feels as if we were all made of one flesh.

When we drank our breakfast coffee, you said you went to see two movies in the afternoon and spent the evening watching the fight at our friends' house, and that you talked with them a long time, and walked all the way back from the Village at three o'clock in the morning, in the freezing cold, and that it had felt good.

Were you there with her, I asked you, my voice low and steady. No, you said. And I believed you. When you see her you don't volunteer any information about what you do. It's another code between us. Silence = Betrayal. Silence = Her.

So when I was driving past her house you weren't there, you were not making love to her, you were at the movies. I sighed in relief. When was the last time you had spent your whole Saturday on your own?

Are we back at square one? I don't believe events turn around. They march forward, unfolding, feelings popping up at the surface and being removed like scum, while deeper conflicts and fears emerge.

Are you actually looking at both of us, wondering which woman is the one for you? Like in a shoe store, hesitating between a pair of boots and a pair of loafers? I know what you would do with the shoes. You'd buy both pairs. But between two women? Nobody makes a decision cold-bloodedly like that. Are you waiting for one of us to make a move, for one of us to snap, to make a mistake, or a final gesture? Are you waiting for one of us to dump you? To lose her nerve? Are we—she and I—so much alike that neither of us is losing her cool, neither of us will put pressure on you?

You are mute about your relationship with her. I can only guess that you two communicate by e-mail, that you make yourself available to her when she's free, or when there's some event planned. Unless there's something planned here, or I ask you to stay in the evening for Lola.

Why is it that you find yourself with two women who are both willing to accept you no matter what you do, no matter how much you go back and forth? Or is your desirability heightened by the fact that we are in competition for you? If one of us were to let you go, would the situation deflate like a balloon?

One hears about adultery in a loveless marriage. How there was no love, no sensuality between the husband and wife. It isn't like that between us. You couldn't—you still cannot—touch me without wanting to make love to me. Our lives have always been a furious combination of sex, writing, and children's laughs and cries. I thought we had the perfect life, crazy and unstable, I thought passion and unpredictability were the key to our relationship. Made it all work. I still don't understand. I'm afraid I've failed you. In some deep way that I don't know. When I found out about your affair, you told me: things have been over between us for years.

Over between us for years? What was over?

The friendship, you said. With her it's not about sex, it's about friendship.

But I thought I was your best friend. One time a couple of years ago, at a party after a friend's opening, you told me you'd love to leave and go to South America. And when I bristled, afraid to lose you, already, you kissed me and said, who can I tell about these desires if not you, my best friend? And I cherished that moment. I was sorry to have felt so threatened.

Everybody says how strong the bond still seems to be between us. How connected we still obviously are. She knew that too. She saw us together.

I'm sentimental tonight. I've drunk a martini at a party and come back early to put Lola to bed, because she asked me.

When I go to parties men come to me, but I don't feel anything. I think it's because I'm still in love with you, because I am still your woman.

I will have to break up with you to be able to have another man.

—————

*Y*ou're going to LA next week, you tell me. To try to get some movie work. I am surprised at first, because your agent said you didn't need to go. Maybe you've decided to get out of town and take a break from everything, take some distance.

You keep everything in so tightly I am reduced to interpreting signs. I try to make sense of the patterns of your moves and silences and rare words, like the Delphic oracle, sitting on a tripod over the fumes.

Why don't you say anything to me about what's going on with you, about what you're feeling right now, I ask you.

You are silent for a while.

I am afraid I would give you hope if I started to talk to you, you say.

Even that statement is ambiguous.

Do you mean to say you'd feel closer to me?

You say you don't know. But that sometimes when you talk you get carried away. You say things you don't mean.

So you remain silent.

The prisoner has the right to remain silent.

Your silence is treacherous.

You are standing at the kitchen counter pouring fresh hot coffee into the thermos, about to go upstairs to your office to write, when I ask you if you are going to LA on your own or if she's going with you.

Your back is to me, the steaming mug of coffee in front of you.

You wait a beat.

I'm going with her.

The stiletto goes right in. It doesn't hurt as much now. The wound is numb. It's as if there are holes in my chest already open for your stabs.

You try to soften the blow: she's going for work, you say. I decided to go at the same time.

$\mathcal{I}$ didn't tell you how upset I was. To me it felt as if you were flaunting your affair in my face. I felt the rage come up, but I didn't know what to do with it.

I guess I could have said stupid words like: PACK UP YOUR BAGS AND GET THE FUCK OUT OF HERE, I NEVER WANT TO SEE YOUR FUCKING FACE AGAIN IN MY LIFE. I AM SORRY I EVER MET YOU AND HAD TWO CHIL-DREN WITH YOU. DROP DEAD, YOU AND YOUR LOW-LIFE BITCH.

$\mathcal{I}$ don't say those words. They lie in my mouth like sick dogs. Instead I decide to spend the weekend out of town, and when I tell you about my plans in the evening, right before you are "going out," I can see you bristle with anger, maybe because that means you have to take care of the kids. For once. Instead of doing whatever the fuck you want to do. For once I am not going to be your fucking babysitter. Your maid. I don't care if you're angry. I don't care anymore.

$\mathcal{I}$ leave the car to you and rent one for myself and drive out on Friday night to my friends' country house in the first flurries of snow. I am so furious I could drive fifteen hours straight through an ice storm. On the country road the snow comes at me in pellets of sleet hitting the windshield. The wipers are useless.

The four walls of the car press in on me, and it's too hot, suddenly. I sweat and lean forward to see the cone of road in the headlights.

Our sexual fantasies always meshed, but our emotional fantasies lately crosswired: I thought I was in a passionate love affair with you, and you thought you were in a bad marriage. Maybe I needed the fantasy of the love affair to get me through the last two years of evenings when you sullenly watched the ballgames sprawled on the couch, and the dinners when you snapped at Juliet or complained about Lola's whine and furiously tossed your plate in the sink.

And yet: your smile, when you held my waist in your hands and pressed me against you, your hunger, running your hands all over me, your loving attention when you read my work—you've always been my best reader—your constant encouragement. These are also undeniable. Your tenderness moved me to tears when you brought me breakfast in bed on Sunday mornings, scones and fresh bialys laid out on the blue tray you bought for me in London. Your thoughtfulness when you built a wall-to-wall bookcase in my study, for my birthday three years ago, a surprise I discovered when I flew back from France, after the summer.

The snow falling is so thick I drive at ten miles per hour. It's been three and a half hours that I've been on the road—a trip that was supposed to last two hours, tops. It feels like I'm moving through a rain of powdered sugar. I put the wipers on now but they don't help very much.

A few years ago I dreamed that you had changed the apartment around. The baby grand piano had been pushed against a door, supporting a kind of scaffolding, a second refrigerator had been brought up and stood in the middle of the hallway. The staircase was blocked. Friends of yours had left behind furniture and objects that filled up the rooms. The apartment felt tiny. I was suffocating. In the dream I told you that I couldn't stand living here if you didn't get rid of all the junk.

Maybe we were both suffocating together. Maybe neither of us knew how to get rid of our junk, maybe we let it all pile up until we couldn't breathe.

I think about you in LA taking her to Venice, where you and I fell in love. I think about you and her walking on the boardwalk, hand in hand, like we used to do. We would walk side by side and we would talk. I would listen to your dreams. They were infectious. You had big dreams. I don't mean dreams of fame and fortune, although you had those dreams too. The dreams that fascinated me were those of your imagination. You took me into your fantasy world, and I sank with you. You created a world with your words, in your soft, gentle voice, and I fell in like Alice through the rabbit hole. Your world was shimmering, going there with you was like swimming into deep waters without an oxygen tank, but you kept me alive, miraculously. It wasn't my world, it was yours, and it was a privilege to enter it. Do you let her enter your world too? Will the Venice boardwalk feel the same to you now as it did with me nineteen years ago?

*U*pstate I stumble through the icy snow.

*I*t's my turn, now, to find myself thrown on another shore. Alone in America. Not mediated by you anymore. Face to face with myself. Picking up where I left off nineteen years ago. Is every love affair a side trip from oneself? But I am not the same now as I was then. I became a woman with you. I became a writer. It was your gift to me.

I hear she likes to watch baseball and football on TV like you do. Instead of steamy sex on Sunday afternoons, maybe the two of you lounge around on her couch, in socks, munching Doritos and pistachio nuts and slapping your thighs in unison at the latest touchdown. She gets me, you say, we share the same culture. Maybe she reminds you of the popular girl you lusted after in high school. And now that you've become the coolest guy in the class, you finally get your dreamgirl.

When I come back from the country it's Super Bowl Sunday and you're not home. Only the girls are here, waiting for me. You must be watching football at her place. The first thing Juliet says when I walk in is this:

Mom, Dad took Lola to her place on Saturday night. I was watching TV and Dad and Lola walked in at two o'clock in the morning and Lola showed me these books. She said: look, she gave me these books.

That's what Juliet tells me.

I'm standing at the stove, preparing dinner. I feel the rage and the terror come up simultaneously. How you constantly hit below the belt. How you don't play by the same rules as me. How you don't play by any rule. Were you using Lola to retaliate upon me, because by going away for the weekend I was upsetting your plans? Or was there some other reason that I don't understand?

Are you, by taking Lola to her place, letting me know that our breakup is a done deal, a fait accompli?

Juliet came behind me and put her arms around my waist. Leaned her head against my shoulder.

I'm sorry, Mom, she whispered.

From the couch, Lola said in a syrupy-not-so-innocent voice:

She brushed my hair and I had cupcake and ice-cream for dessert.

Then she showed me the books: there were two Dr. Seuss, two Babar, and a pop-up book you can open and stand on its side.

Lola set up the book and showed me how it worked.

Look, Mom, look, she said.

It looked like a street with shops, and little paper props you can arrange in every shop.

I wanted to throw up. I looked at Lola's hair. It looked unwashed and full of tangles. She hadn't even done a good job of brushing, I thought, nastily.

You came back during the night and I woke up for a few seconds and the rage swept over me. I rolled over to the other side of the bed and made sure that no part of our bodies touched.

In the morning I told you that you shouldn't have taken Lola to her place, not when you were still living with me. You were drinking your coffee and you got testy.

I'm going to be living there anyway, you said.

The stiletto, in and out. A quick one, this time.

You're not living there now, I said. And even if you were, I don't want you to take Lola there, not for a while, not until things settle down. Not until you know what you're doing.

I left the room. I was afraid of your anger. Or maybe of my own.

You went upstairs to get ready. You were going to a press luncheon with her, and the two of you would go straight to the airport from there.

A couple of hours later you appeared at the door of my office wearing a pair of black socks, white boxers, a sports jacket and a sheepish smile. You were carrying two pairs of pants and shoes and another jacket.

Which jacket, do you think?

You looked like a teenage boy asking his older sister what to wear for his first real date. I wanted to slap you in the face. But I stayed cool and gave you sartorial advice and went back to my writing. A half hour later you were all dressed up and carrying your bag and ready to go. You said good-bye to me at the door. I didn't get up from my desk.

$\mathcal{I}$ had already decided I would ask you to leave when you come back from LA.

————————

$\mathcal{A}$ll week I have thought of the moment. I have rehearsed the words in my head. I thought you'd come back in the middle of the night, and I was planning to let you take the kids to school in the morning and tell you as soon as you got back home. The words I kept repeating in my head were these:

The trip to LA was the last straw. You're flaunting your affair in my face. I can't take it anymore. You took Lola to her place. It was like betraying me all over again. I want you to leave. I want you to leave right now. I want you to leave today. Right now.

I imagined you would get testy, you would say something like this: I'm leaving anyway. Or: I was planning to leave anyway. And I would drop the final line:

I want you to leave now.

No matter what would come before, it always ended with:

I want you to leave now.

I stayed awake at night repeating the words, convinced that if I didn't know them by heart I would forget them, I would stumble, I would not say them at all, I would stay speechless.

NOW. RIGHT NOW. I WANT YOU TO LEAVE RIGHT NOW.

Afraid that if I missed the word NOW you would stay until the night and I would have to see you leaving again to go to her.

It was that image of you: putting on your leather jacket and your hat and going to the door, the sound of the door slamming behind you. It was that scene that I didn't want to witness again. Never again.

You called several times from LA and each time I was cold to you. I had never been cold like that to you. I was always seductive. Maybe out of fear that if I didn't seduce you I would lose you. I was cold because I didn't want you to seduce me back, like you always do.

You didn't come back the Sunday night you were supposed to. You called to say you'd stay three more days.

On Wednesday evening I went out for a drink with a friend and rehearsed the words with her. She asked me: are you going to make love to him when he comes back in the middle of the night? I said I would sleep on the other side of the bed. She said, maybe he should sleep in another bed. Make him sleep in the guest room.

I thought about that for a while. Throw you out of our bed. But I wanted to feel your body for the last time, smell your smell, run my hands up the underside of your arms and pin your palms over your head. I wanted to stretch my body over yours, feel you stir between my legs. I knew that by asking you to leave I'd have to give up the touch of your skin on my skin, of your lips on my lips.

One last time, I said.

But I knew I couldn't kick you out if I touched you.

The night of Wednesday to Thursday I woke up at 2 A.M. and I knew—as I had known all the other times—that you weren't going to spend the night. All I thought about was that you had gone straight to her place from the airport and I wouldn't be able to tell you to leave.

On Thursday morning you walk in at 7 A.M., wearing your fedora and carrying your bag, while we're having breakfast.

I took the red-eye, you say. Didn't I tell you?

I'd forgotten the red-eye gets in in the morning.

You put your bag down and pull out gifts wrapped in colorful ribbons. The girls are excited, even Juliet who is so morose these days. Lola's cheeks are flushed, as if it were Christmas all over again. There are presents for the three of us. Clothes for your women, as always. Carefully chosen for style and size. A ponytail holder with a tiny teddy bear for Lola. Once again you are the loving husband and father bearing presents—maybe hoping to be forgiven.

The jeans you give me are orange in shiny sateen and they fit me perfectly. I put them on and wait for you to come back from taking the girls to school. Wait in ambush.

I've decided to tell you as soon as you walk in.

I have something to tell you, I say, and I see on your face that you've already figured it out.

You keep your face blank.

I hear my voice drop, not angry but sad, charged.

The LA trip was the last straw for me. That and taking Lola to her place. I think it showed real bad judgment on your part. I can't stand seeing you leave this house one more time to go to her. The sexual jealousy is unbearable.

You look at me for a second and avert your eyes.

I am getting nothing from you. Five percent of good stuff, sex and a little tenderness. The rest is pure torture. I don't want to be tortured anymore. This is turning into an S&M relationship.

You flinch at that.

S&M, you repeat angrily.

You turn away and pick up your keys.

Okay, you say.

NOW. Now is the time to say it:

I'd like you to move out today.

You don't say anything. You act real pissed off. You put your leather jacket on, ready to flee once again. Then you realize that this time it's for good. You put your keys down.

Your bag is on the floor, still unpacked.

I walk to the window, watch the street. I listen to you gathering some things upstairs, your computer, some books.

I try to imagine what it's going to feel like afterward. I know you're going to go straight to her and live with her. You said you didn't want to take your own apartment because you didn't have the money, and you'd be at her place all the time anyway. I try to figure out what I'm feeling. Pain or relief. But I feel numb. Nineteen years of my life are collapsing in front of me and I have no idea what it means.

The scene's been so short, so slight. So fast. I look at my watch. 9:15 A.M. The whole thing hasn't lasted ten minutes. Fewer than ten minutes to pass to the other side of my life. I think about giving birth. That the last pushes only last a few minutes too.

When you come down I hand you the booklet I have picked up at the post office, "The Mover's Guide" with the change of address form.

Here, I say. I picked that up for you so that you don't have to come everyday to pick up your mail.

Thanks, you reply, as if I was doing you a favor.

I thought I was doing *myself* a favor so that you would stay out of the house.

I go into my office. I don't want to see you get ready. I wonder if you are packing more stuff or if you will just take the bag you took to LA with you. After a while you poke your head in the door and tell me you're going to the post office.

The girls still don't know anything. You haven't talked to them. Lola will be heartbroken when she finds out.

On my desk is the manuscript of the memoir I wrote after meeting my father for the first time last year. At the end of our lunch my father had said: "I am a poor guy, a loser." I think he meant: you didn't miss anything, I couldn't measure up. It was my failure, not yours. I think he meant: don't ask me to answer to you.

The same words you had once said to me, when I had asked who you were having lunch with: I don't want to answer to you.

Maybe I tried to make you my father. In our sexual life I was the one in control, but in our daily life I think you liked to play the role of the older brother, the responsible one, the one in command, the powerful one. You took it over willingly. And I let you do it, maybe because I felt that was the way you wanted to love me, or was it the way I needed to be loved? And then, one day, you got sick of the role. It had become a straitjacket.

You must be disappointed in me, my father had said.

Maybe you're thinking the same thing. That you didn't live up to my expectations, or to your own. But I think your expectations were too high.

And I am thinking that it wasn't just your failure, but mine too.

And that I still love you.

And that I am letting you go.

And that I am whole no matter what you do.

On the walls in my office I taped two drawings made by

Lola: one, with two abstract shapes, titled: *Two Apples*. The other, figurative, showing a redheaded girl holding her skirt up and furiously dancing next to a blurry red figure. That one is titled *Power Girls*. From now on I will be a power girl too.

*O*utside it's a beautiful, mild February day. This weekend Lola and Juliet will be six and sixteen, respectively. You will be here for their birthdays. We'll celebrate them together.

When you come back from the post office I hear you sigh. I have no idea what you are feeling because your initial burst of anger has covered whatever conflicted emotions you may have.

You look determined and busy, cool, maybe relieved that I've finally taken action.

You say: I'll have to organize myself. I can't do it all in one day.

I'm sorry it's so abrupt, I say. That's the only way I can do this.

Your bag is still on the floor in the hallway. Zipped up now—I don't think you've packed anything else in it—and your computer bag next to it. You didn't even take a shower.

Tonight I will put on the new sheets.

*Y*ou're about to leave. You've put on your leather jacket and your black cap, and I am wearing the orange sateen jeans you brought me. We're standing face to face.

You take me into your arms and hug me tight. My face is into your neck. We stay in each other's arms without speaking for a long time. When we pull away, you say, I won't kiss you, I'm coming down with a cold.

I didn't want to kiss you anyway, I say, but I did.

Do you know what we're doing? I ask you.

No.

Me neither.

I feel tears in my eyes and I choke them up.

They are still our daughters and we are still us, I tell you.

Yes, you say.

You let go of me and pick up your bag, sling your computer bag over your shoulder.

I watch you leave from the door. I watch you walk down the stairs. You look up to me before getting to the lower landing. But you're wearing your shades and I can't see your eyes. I feel the density of the unspoken between us.

We do not say good-bye.

Not a word.

This is not a good-bye. It is what it is: you walking out of our house to go to her place. There's no word for that. No label. We do not know what it means.

There are things that cannot be said. You and I are not good at saying what we feel. Only at putting it in images and scenes. Your last novel was telling me where you were at. When you were reading each chapter in bed to me before we made love, you were confessing to me, in a way. And this journal is my response to you.

So you left me after all. Maybe not today but a year and a half ago, without telling me. You pretended everything was as it had been. Your mind slipped out the back door and your body stayed with me, in our bed. And I couldn't tell. Maybe I knew, but I couldn't face it. I stuck my head in the sand because it was too painful to contemplate. Because I would have had to rage at you, and I would have been too scared to confront you.

But now that you are gone I am no longer scared to lose you.

*E*very other day you come to see the kids or for some business in the house. You always call before coming. Mainly you come to be with them when I go out. They are happy to see you but it's harder when you leave.

*W*hen I first told Lola, the day you left, she screamed out of anger and panic and I had to call you at your new place. You had written the phone number on a pad and I dialed. It shook me up to do that. I hoped that she would be in her office, not at home with you, answering the phone. From now on I couldn't call you freely. I'd be your ex. You would be another woman's man, you wouldn't even have your own phone line, nor your own address. Her home was your home now.

You answered on the first ring.

We met you at the children's playground where I had given you rendezvous. Lola didn't want to play. We had a hot chocolate in a café and you and I comforted her. We told her that you would be living in the apartment Lola had visited the previous Saturday night, and that you would see her a lot. Little by little she calmed down.

Juliet already knew. I had told her the evening before that I would ask you to leave. She was prepared for it.

At dinner, we tried to talk about what had happened but it was too hard. Juliet wanted to be alone and call her friends.

I put the new sheets on the bed and slept like a stone.

*N*ow it's just the three of us but you're still here like a ghost.

Juliet mostly stares at the TV. Lola gets upset. She asks me: am I divorced, Mom? She has trouble going to sleep, tosses and turns in her bed, and kicks and talks as if she were on speed. You tell me she has no trouble going to sleep when you put her to bed. You want her to go to your new place but I think it's way too early, too painful, for me and for her too. You tell me I am selfish. You asked Juliet if she would want to meet your girlfriend and she said no. It must be hard for you too. You come here and cook for them, tomato sauce or chicken soup like you used to, wearing an oversize T-shirt and a pair of sweatpants, and I imagine what it must feel like for you to be here, although you don't say anything about it. You keep your face blank and talk to the girls with great love.

When I leave for a date all dressed up and made up, I lean over the couch and I touch you lightly on the knee or the arm, on the fabric, not on the bare skin, and you look sad, or blank, as if you were trying not to see me. I still don't really know how we got where we are. Sometimes there's this wave of tenderness between us, and you hug me tight and kiss me on the lips when you leave. Sometimes my rage spills out of my mouth like slimy toads. Now that you have left, I can finally let it out.

One morning you came because Juliet had been crying, and you decided to take her out for a ride to the Cloisters on your motorcycle. I couldn't contain my fury. I accused you of fucking up the girls, of deliberately breaking us up because you wanted to be bad and a rebel and you didn't give a fuck. You yelled back at me. You said I fucked them up because I have a father problem. Usually you say I have a mother problem. This was a new one.

Then, out of the blue, you fired your ultimate weapon, the atomic bomb:

It's over between us, you said.

As if I hadn't gotten it. Yet.

Yeah, I said. Sarcastic, dripping with venom. A giant toad balanced at the edge of my tongue. It's over between us.

Remember? I kicked you out two weeks ago.

I feel the rage come up in deep waves like when you are going to vomit and you can't hold it anymore, you kneel over the curb and throw it all up, whole chunks of carrots, skins of tomatoes, undigested morsels of steak, all bathing in a green bile.

I'm glad we broke up, I yell. I wouldn't have broken up what we had, but it's the best thing that's ever happened to me.

I see your face fall.

Touché.

I am not afraid anymore.

You walk out of the bathroom and go upstairs.

Then I notice that Juliet is sitting on the toilet quietly crying, her hands over her face, and Lola starts hitting me.

Stop it, she screams, stop it.

It's not true that stories climax and resolve. It's only true in the make-believe world of fiction. In the real world stories get told over and over, like a Möbius knot.

When you come back in the afternoon we make up and the air clears again and the tenderness comes back and I can see there is no end in sight. No end to this story.

No end at all.

The students at Rutgers University, where I am teaching creative writing this semester, wear baggy pants, oversize T-shirts, and carry themselves with that slouch. The same way you carry yourself. Teenage-man even now. When I check men out in the street to see which ones turn me on, it's always the twenty-year-olds, the thirty-year-olds, that I want.

Maybe they arouse in me a perverse maternal instinct. Maybe you aroused that in me too. When you would rest your face on my breasts and take a nipple into your mouth and I held you between my arms, were you my son or my father? With your daughters you're a pal, or a Jewish mother cooking chicken soup.

I don't know what a man is. To me you were it. You were my man. You were the man.

You come back to the house all the time. Sometimes I think I hear the keys in the door and I expect to see you come in, tall silhouette and leather jacket filling the narrow hallway. But you're not here. There's only silence and the hollow sounds of an empty house.

And sometimes it's you. You really are coming in the door, and I see your face and it looks sick to me, like a distorted shadow of the former face that I loved, that I held in my hands so many times. Your face looks gray and sepia-brown, like the colors you usually wear, as if you had just stepped out of an old black and white movie.

The day before your birthday, it's a Friday, you come to babysit for Lola, because I am going to a party and Juliet is out, sleeping over at a friend's. I am getting ready to go out when you walk into the bedroom.

I suppose you won't let me take the girls out to the restaurant with her for my birthday tomorrow?

Your question goes straight to my heart, another dagger, no, a poison arrow this time, shot from those Indian blowguns you brought back from Ecuador, which are hanging above the staircase. Your tone is that of a pissed-off teenager who knows it's no use asking permission to go out on Saturday night but who tries anyway.

I am sitting on the bed, sewing a button on a jacket.

No, I say, you can't. It's way too early.

I am speaking coldly, like a stern mother. But what I want to say is HOW DO YOU DARE EVEN THINK OF REPLACING ME WITH HER WHAT FUCKING NERVE YOU NEVER

USED TO TAKE THE GIRLS OUT FOR YOUR BIRTHDAY
WHEN WE WERE TOGETHER WHAT'S GOT INTO YOU
TO MAKE YOUR BIRTHDAY A FAMILY OUTING WITH
HER.

I don't say any of that. I am cold cold cold and I go on sewing the button as if I were in control of the situation and I say, not yet, I am not ready yet, I don't think Lola is ready yet either, let's wait until after the summer.

You storm out of the bedroom, pissed off.

I keep all of my feelings tied up in a bundle under the cool exterior and I leave to go to the party, but when I get there, after one glass of wine, all the feelings come unraveled and I have to go out and sob in the street, sitting on a stoop on Great Jones Street, my head between my arms, hoping nobody will recognize me.

When I come back home it's 2 A.M. and you are in a funk.

I'll never do this again, you say, threateningly, lacing up your boots at the kitchen table. Next time get a sitter. You got some nerve to come back at two o'clock in the morning.

I'm sorry, I say. I wasn't paying attention to the time.

I hope you had a great time, you say, your teeth clenched.

I think maybe you imagine I was fucking some guy and you're jealous, so I give you a wry smile and say, in a chipper voice, yeah, actually, I had a great time. Even though I was miserable all evening.

I don't know what sets you off exactly, is it what I just said, or because I finally got angry and I asked you why you still hadn't removed your stuff from the apartment? Or because I won't let the girls celebrate your birthday tomorrow with you and your girlfriend?

Your anger must have been simmering since the early evening, when I stood up to you. Or maybe it was the culmination of all those years of frustration with my neediness, my self-involvement, with your own shortcomings, with the pressures of raising a family, with our failure to make it all work, with the power I still have over you.

You have left me, but I can still pull the strings, I can still control you. Maybe that's what sets you off, that you cannot make a clean break, that we will be forever entangled.

I don't know.

One time you told me—it was one of our earlier conversations—that you felt trapped.

You created this family, this home with me, and it became a trap because you couldn't just walk away from it without enormous guilt and shame. On one level, you are a man of principle, a family man, a generous man. But you are also a hothead, impulsive, you don't know how to keep your cool. When the pressure builds, you blow a fuse, you pick a fight. How many times did I see you on the verge of punching a guy in the face in the street, or cutting a car on the highway?

There's a wild streak in you. When your system short-circuits you lose control, you see red. You call it the red haze.

Now you move into the red haze zone.

I see it before you even make your move.

Right after I tell you I want you to remove all your furniture and your clothes from the apartment, your face tightens and you grab me by the arm. Your eyes machine-gun me, black, spilling raw hate.

I'm going to kill you. I'M GOING TO FUCKING KILL YOU.

Calm down, I say, calm down, but you toss me on the ground and drag me across the floor, still holding on to my arm in a vise-grip.

You let go of me and I jump up in a fury.

Are you insane?

FUCK YOU. FUCK YOU!

You march toward the laundry room and tear the accordion doors off their hinges, toss them across the hallway.

Then you come back holding a ladder with both your hands and threaten to hit me with it.

Adrenaline is running too fast for me to feel scared. I don't believe you would lose control all the way and try to kill me. Not deliberately. I believe you could hurt me, but that I can calm you down, like I've always done.

You drop the ladder and grab the cats' scratching pole, which is anchored on a square wooden platform, and hit the wall with the wooden part as if it were an axe, over and over until you've made a deep gash in the Sheetrock. You look like a madman turned wolfman with green hair and fangs, one of those comic book characters whose repressed primitive nature emerges once a month and starts howling at the full moon.

This time I am scared. I run to my office and try to lock myself in, but the lock's busted and I call the friends I was with at the party to tell them what's going on, so that they know, in case you continue with your rampage.

I grew up with violence. My mother used to throw pots and pans and furniture around when she felt trapped or humiliated. The two of us lived with my grandparents, and she had no control over her life. When the tensions mounted, cursing and banging things around and storming out of the house were the only ways she knew how to let out steam. You, it's always the wall that you attack. Like that time when you grabbed a chair by its back and plowed through the kitchen wall with the back feet. We had a good laugh about it afterward. There were two gaping holes in the Sheetrock for months, until we had the kitchen redone. You told me that you had gotten so angry at something or someone once that you had grabbed a glass table and thrown the glass top on the ground. You had loved the sound of shattering glass, it had been a big kick.

I don't know if you're getting a kick out of this.

After a long time, maybe twenty minutes, everything quiets down. Lola, who could sleep through an air raid, hasn't stirred.

When I come out of my office I see you are gathering some tools to re-hang the laundry room door. I watch you for a while.

I think you should go home now, I tell you.

I'll go home when I want to, you say.

I go upstairs to sleep while you're still fixing the damage.

The next morning when I come down for breakfast I find you with a trowel and a bucket of joint compound, plastering the gaping hole in the wall.

Is your violence a measure of your pain? Of your despair? Of your helplessness? Of your regrets, perhaps? Of everything that you cannot express and that chokes you?

Your violence tells me something about your love and your shame. But the language is so crude it's hard for me to understand it clearly.

What I am hearing is this: that you will never completely forgive yourself, or me, for the failure of our relationship. That it will always, in some way, eat at you. That you really tried as hard as you could to make this life with me, against enormous odds, and that it breaks your heart that we failed.

You are an idealist, a dreamer. Perhaps more than I am.

You tried so hard, you said. You did the best you could.

———

I know I cannot hold on to the girls forever. I want them to see you freely. I have to let them go to her place on weekends if they want to. It is the hardest part. I have fought against it for a month, but you keep putting pressure on me to let Lola go and see where you live.

You're selfish, you tell me. You only think about yourself.

Lola cries to you on the phone: I want to go see your house, Dada, she says. Inside I cringe. What it feels like to me is this: not only do I have to give you up, but I have to share my daughters with her too. Why do I have to give up so much? I feel the hand of fate squeezing me like a lemon, forcing me to cough up what I've got, as if I had had too much, as if I were hoarding it selfishly.

Maybe I am. I am an only child. I haven't learned how to share. I tend to cling to what I have, afraid that it will be taken away from me.

You try to reassure me. You say: she won't be Lola's mother. You will always be the mother. She will be her friend.

I cringe even more. You say the word "friend" with a certain tone, filling your mouth up with air, as if you were anointing her with the sacrament of that word, a friend being higher in your set of values than a lover, friendship higher than sex. Anyway, now she is going to be Lola and Juliet's friend. And who am I to deny them a wonderful and warm new friend?

A friend who bought Lola a pair of Winnie the Pooh sheets to put on the futon in your office, and stickers and Beanie Babies, and drew little hearts pierced with arrows on pink paper when Lola went to see you last Sunday. I want to dip them in vitriol.

I finally decide to let Lola spend the weekend at her place. Or should I say "your" place? The more I wait, the more you will put pressure on me. I don't want the girls to be caught in a tug-of-war between us.

I offer to drive Lola to you on Saturday night, since she's too young to ride on your motorcycle. I'm not sure why I'm doing that. Not to save you cab fare, that's for sure. But there's a certain power in driving her, symbolically depositing her in your trust at the moment of my choice. I'd rather do it myself than have you come to the apartment and take her away. I think I want to face the moment head-on, experience it firsthand. Prove to myself that I am strong enough to take it. I feel cocky, I think. I'm over you. I can handle it.

I turn the corner of her block, I ease past the convent door, I pull up in front of the green door. You're supposed to be there waiting for me but you're not. I didn't want to call first, so we have agreed on a time for me to drop Lola off.

I ring her bell—top buzzer, tiny black dot, her name next to it, not your name. There's no answer. I ring again after a little while, expecting to hear you. And all of a sudden I hear her voice, her naked voice, calling me from above. I look up to see her in the evening shadows, leaning out of a window.

Catherine, she calls. And I can't believe she's calling my name in the street, shattering the fragile protection I have surrounded myself with, collapsing, in that one word, the distance I have put between her and me. My name in her mouth feels obscene.

Catherine! Wait a minute. He's on his way down.

It's a nothing moment. Insignificant. How many times have I called a friend from my window when my intercom wasn't working? But I'm not her friend. And it's not a nothing moment for me. I am bringing Lola to her for the first time. I have to trust her with Lola, because you have chosen her as your new woman. It's a violent moment for me, this voluntary surrender that I am accomplishing for your sake and Lola's sake. And she's making me feel my surrender, talking down to me from her turf, high up on her second or third floor window, I can't quite tell because her head went back in and I don't look up anymore, I lean against the wall, shivering.

Just then you appear at the door. You sense something's up right away.

What's wrong? you ask.

I am shaking with rage. But I don't know what's wrong. Only that I feel violated and provoked.

But I can't tell you that. Not like that.

Next time be here, is all I can manage to say.

*O*n Sunday afternoon you bring Lola back. I am nervous. I wonder how she will be after spending her first night at your place. You took her to see *Star Wars*. She babbles on about her weekend. I imagine the three of you in the theater, the three of you holding hands in the street, Lola between you two, like a happy family, like we used to be years ago, except you've replaced me with her.

And then, after you leave, Lola says: last night I had dinner with Dada's friend's parents.

When she hears about the dinner with the parents, Juliet calls you on the phone to yell at you. She feels betrayed. She is sobbing when she hangs up.

Later Lola calls her house and talks to her. Juliet and I both listen in on the conversation. Now it's Lola the traitor, Lola the turncoat. Juliet refuses to speak to her sister for the rest of the evening.

*T*his weekend, while you are out with Lola and Juliet, your British editor calls. He needs to change his dinner plans with you. As soon as I realize she has given him my phone number, that she has told him to call here, as soon as I hear her name, I turn cold and curt.

There had been one previous phone call.

She called me herself.

It was just a few days ago, Tuesday or Wednesday of last week, one morning when you had come over to drive Juliet and Lola to school. It was about 9 A.M. She had locked herself in, she told me, and couldn't get out of her apartment to go to work. She couldn't find her keys. Or maybe you had her keys, I don't know. Maybe she, too, is losing her keys like you used to lose yours. In any case, she needed you to unlock her door right away. You were not back from school yet, so I took the message. My heart started to beat too fast, and I was overwhelmed with anger but I choked it down. I was cool but polite. She was polite but abrupt.

Her voice had the same tone as when she had called my name from her window. Casual, but with an undertow of command and maybe even provocation. Her casualness felt aggressive, as if she was denying—again—the violence of what was taking place among the three of us. She was summoning you back to her chambers, where you belonged, and by asking me to convey the message to you, she was in effect erasing me, reducing me to the role of messenger between you and her.

This time, too, my heart is pounding after I hang up with your British editor. I am seething with rage. So there are no boundaries, no respect for my feelings. Again I feel the casualness of giving my phone number to this man, your editor—as if we are all friends helping each other out, as if nothing has happened in our lives, as if she has nothing to do with it—is coarse and insensitive. Business first, no matter what. Business as usual.

But maybe these phone calls—and especially the first one—are not pure casualness on her part but covert acts of aggression. Maybe she is angry that you are still coming here and spending time at my place. Maybe this is her way of letting me know that you are hers and she has the right to get in touch with you wherever you are, especially about your work, which is her business—even if it hurts me.

Of course, I might be looking for a moment like that. The tiniest gesture is bound to set me off.

Maybe I am looking for it.

I don't know. I'm not thinking that clearly. I only feel a blind rage. I let it build to boiling point, which takes about five minutes, and I dial her number.

It's Catherine, I say, when she picks up the phone.

This time I haven't rehearsed. I just let the words pour out of my mouth.

I don't want you to call here, I say. I don't want you to call this house, ever. I don't want you to give this phone number to anyone.

It was his British editor, she says. He needs to get in touch with him urgently. It's about his book.

I don't care, I say. I don't want to hear your voice. I don't want to hear your name. I don't want to hear about you. The only way you may ever call here is if there's a real emergency, like somebody has had an accident or somebody died.

Yes, ma'am, she says.

My heart is still pounding when I hang up, but I am relieved that I have finally told her off, that ghost you are living with. In that alternate reality you share with her.

That ghost I cannot bear to bring to life.

When I meet you later outside McDonald's, where I am supposed to pick up the girls and take them back home, you already know about the phone incident. Dark furrows of anger are lining your forehead. You take me aside.

What the fuck did you think you were doing? you say. It was

my British editor. He had to get in touch with me to change our dinner plans.

I don't care, I say. She can't call here. She can't give my phone number to anyone. It's off-limits.

It's my phone number too. People have a right to call me at this number. Change the fucking phone number if you don't like it!

No, I won't. It's *my* phone number now. You don't live with me anymore.

You're out of your mind, you say.

———

*W*ay before you left, during the fall, when I was imagining what it would be like to be on my own, I had decided to throw a big party when you left. I didn't know why exactly. Survival instinct, I guess. To assert to the world that I wasn't a dejected/rejected ex-wife, but a free, single woman. I planned the party as soon as you left. It was going to be a week after your birthday. You overheard me mention it at Lola's birthday party.

Are you having a party for my birthday without inviting me? you asked.

Yes. It's going to be in your honor, in memoriam.

You smirked.

It was the first time I was having a big blowout party by myself in our apartment. I was going to walk the path we had so many times walked together: the candles, the glasses, the booze, the food, the music, but on my own, without you. I had a pair of speakers wired upstairs in your ex-office, which made it part of the scene. Your big, airy office would be a dance floor for my own pleasure. It would be like dancing on your grave.

The party was meant as the kickoff of my new life. It was packed. It went on all night. It was exhilarating. A kind of exorcism. I was reclaiming my sexuality on the turf of our love. The very place where we had loved and hurt each other. A public ritual is very powerful. I performed it with the ferocious energy of life feasting over a still-warm corpse. I barely had to lift a finger. Everybody had come to celebrate with me. A week before, I had bought a secondhand Isaac Mizrahi poppy-red stretch dress with spaghetti straps. I had carefully chosen the dress: the style, and the color. I had wanted a red dress. Nothing short of red would have done. The dress worked its magic.

By 6 A.M. the next morning, when everybody had finally left, and I fell asleep in the new sheets, the ritual was completed. And, for the first time since I met you, I had made love with another man.

*O*ur couple had finally bit the dust.

Le Roi est mort. Vive le Roi.

———

*W*hen you brought me your fresh-off-the-press novel the morning I was going to leave for Paris, I realized, as I looked at the flap copy, that you had omitted my name as coeditor of the magazine we edit together. I finally—finally—lashed out at you without holding back. I raged at you from the hallway, cornering you between the door and the washing machine, where you were trying to fix the laundry room door again, the door you had pulled off its hinges a few weeks ago. It keeps falling off.

You are a lowlife egomaniac, I yelled at you. Are you so

insecure you need to erase me from your past to make yourself look better?

You were livid. You went on screwing and hammering and fumbling for screws, your body shaking with rage.

You said "fuck you" many times. You said you stayed with me to take care of me.

You stayed with me because you loved me.

No, I didn't, you said.

I am taking care of myself, finally, you went on.

*W*hy are you trying to eliminate the memory of our love? Does it make it easier for you to create a brand-new persona, without a past? Or is it the only way that you can love someone else?

*I*n the evening, before I left for the airport, you came back. You were going to stay here with the kids while I was in France. You were supposed to have dinner with us but you were pissed. You didn't sit down at the table.

It was your turn to corner me this time and lash back at me. You said many things. The one that I remember is that I was a dysfunctional neurotic.

Juliet was so angry because of our fight that she refused to say good-bye to me. Lola had a temper tantrum.

At the airport the plane was delayed, and I hung out at the bar with two fashion photographers from London. I started to feel better, erasing the memory of the day, of the pain we are inflicting on our daughters.

The next morning you called me in Paris to apologize. You said you had omitted my name on the flap copy of your novel out of anger at me.

I did it on purpose, you said on the phone. I wanted to eliminate you.

I made you promise you would never do that again.

We made up. I was relieved.

𝒟uring the week I spent in Paris on my own, I was so excited by my new freedom, I thought of that Egyptian proverb: "Throw a lucky man in the Nile and he will come back up with a fish in his mouth."

I feel like that man.

———

ℐ have used up all the matches I have found in the house from all the bars that you've been to in the last year (with or without her, I don't know, but certainly without me). I am quickly replacing them with matches culled from the clubs and bars I'm going to now with other men. Men who are not like you, maybe because they are younger and they belong to another generation. Or maybe because they are truly not like you. I don't know really. After nineteen years with one man, making love with another is a little like popping your cherry for the second time.

It's not you that I think of now when I go to sleep at night in the new sheets. I am falling out of love with you.

By letting the hands of another man touch me I am erasing your tracks. Like you tried to eliminate me. Like one removes a tattoo. Your body will not be written on mine anymore. Only the memory will remain. And our daughters, connecting us forever.

———

T met a man. He is very young. Younger than you were when I first met you. Our bodies connected like your body and mine connected. Instantly. Making love with him is heartbreaking. Together we have that spark I thought I would never feel again. But he's been caught by surprise. He wasn't ready for that. One day, on the phone, he tells me: it's not going to work out between us. I don't want him to say that. I still have the memory of his naked arms on my arms, of his hands pressing hard on my stomach, of his blissful smile.

Maybe you're right, I say. Ultimately, it won't last. Relationships end, affairs fall apart. But it doesn't mean that one shouldn't have them. It doesn't mean that one shouldn't fall crazily in love and live.

Passionate love affairs die hard. They convulse and writhe and agonize till the bitter end. But the bliss and the headiness of love is worth the agony of the breakup. Death always comes at the end of life.

What you did, I might have done it too. The details, the sequences, might have been different. I might have been less cruel, more decisive, but sooner or later it would have ended.

T have asked you to remove your clothes and your chest of drawers from our bedroom because I have sublet the apartment for the whole summer. All your clothes are still here, all your books, your desk, your filing cabinets, your Ecuadoran blowgun and poisoned arrows, your record collection. You're still living out of that bag you had taken to LA with you four months ago.

You started packing in the morning, and when I came back

home in the afternoon the chest of drawers was gone and your closet empty save for some lone vests and pants from the seventies. There were bundles of books fastened with twine lined up by the front door. On the pink table was a heap of shirts on their hangers. On top I recognized a couple of flannel shirts in faded colors from almost twenty years ago. Shirts that you were wearing in LA, in Montreal.

I sobbed a little in your arms.

It's hard, I told you.

I thought you were handling this so well, you said, surprised.

It's hard to separate, I said. Isn't it hard for you?

Yes, you said.

And we sat down together at the yellow kitchen table like we used to and we talked.

Your shirts in a pile. Your books in bundles. This is the way you had moved from LA to Montreal. Discarding things quickly, grabbing your clothes in armloads. The way I had moved from Paris to Montreal myself, and then from Montreal to New York. From love affair to love affair. Ours went on for so long, I believed it would last.

$\mathcal{I}$ go into my office to write while you are packing. I describe the shirts in a pile, the books in bundles. The words are stigmata that I'm imprinting on the yellow pad, to bear witness.

So that our life together doesn't vanish without a trace.

So that there will be a record.

New York City,
September 1996—May 1997

Acknowledgments

Thanks to Joy Harris for her faithful loyalty, and to Betsy Lerner for her enthusiasm and fearlessness.

Catherine Texier was born and raised in France and now lives in New York City. Her first novel, *Chloé l'Atlantique,* was written in French and published in Paris. She is the author of two novels in English, *Love Me Tender* and *Panic Blood.* Her work has been translated into nine languages. She was the coeditor, with Joel Rose, of the literary magazine *Between C&D,* and has coedited with him two anthologies of short fiction: *Between C&D* and *Love Is Strange.* She is the recipient of a National Endowment for the Arts Award and a New York Foundation for the Arts Fellowship.